The Incarnation of the Poetic Word

Theological Essays on Poetry & Philosophy
Philosophical Essays on Poetry & Theology

✝

Michael Martin

The Incarnation
of the Poetic Word

✛

Theological Essays
on Poetry & Philosophy

Philosophical Essays
on Poetry & Theology

Foreword by
William Desmond

Afterword by
Therese Schroeder-Sheker

 Angelico Press

First published
by Angelico Press 2017
© Michael Martin 2017
Foreword © William Desmond 2017
Afterword © Therese Schroeder-Sheker 2017

For information, address:
Angelico Press
4709 Briar Knoll Dr.
Kettering, OH 45429
angelicopress.com

978-1-62138-239-3 (pbk)
978-1-62138-240-9 (cloth)
978-1-62138-241-6 (ebook)

Cover design: Michael Schrauzer

CONTENTS

Acknowledgments

A FEW of these essays were first published in other contexts. "Criticism and Contemplation: Steps toward an Agapeic Criticism" first appeared in *Logos: A Journal of Catholic Thought and Culture*, "George Herbert and the Phenomenology of Grace" in *The George Herbert Journal*, and "The Poetic of Sophia" in *The Heavenly Country: An Anthology of Primary Sources, Poetry, and Critical Essays on Sophiology* (Angelico Press, 2016). For their publication I am eternally grateful.

I am likewise indebted to a number of friends and colleagues for their support and valuable insight over the years, especially George Alcser, Steven Patterson, Sarah Heidt, Judith Heinen, James Wetmore, and John Riess. I am also grateful to my assistant, Alejandra Villegas, for her tireless work and special friendship. In addition, I offer my deepest appreciation to William Desmond and Therese Schroeder-Sheker for their grace and generosity in contributing their words to the book. Much love to both of you. Above all I thank my children—Brendan, Dylan, Thomas, Mae, Aidan, Zelie, Isabel, Gabriel, and Daniel—and my wife, Bonnie, who by her very presence constantly witnesses that poetry, philosophy, and theology bear more than theoretical or intellectual importance; and who, in addition, gives constant proof to Guillaume Apollinaire's assertion that it is "*L'amour qui emplit ainsi que la lumière / Tout le solide espace entre les étoiles et les planets.*" This book is dedicated to her.

Foreword

MICHAEL Martin is a poet, a theologian, and a person of philosophical inclination: all of these roles diversely, and all of them communicating with each other in his rich writings. This, his plurivocal vocation, is given diverse expression in *The Incarnation of the Poetic Word*, where he remains true to what he terms the practice of agapeic criticism. The generosity of the agapeic enables, sustains, passes through his poetic, theological and philosophical engagements.

Often when we think of agape we consider it by contrast with other forms of love, such as eros and philia. Thinking in this contrastive way we tend to define agape as over against other forms of love. This is not simply wrong, but we do have the tendency to think of agape then as being in one box, so to say, while other forms of love, such as eros and philia, are in other boxes, in their own boxes. The result is that agape becomes limited by what it is not, boxed in and in a certain sense domesticated by contrast with these other forms of love. Of course, agape cannot be so bound, restricted, finitized, pinned down as just one form of love over against other forms, and so subject to the limitations of exclusive definition. There are no bounds here. There is something unrestricted about agape. It names an unconditional generosity towards all that is, and so signifies not just an openness to the whole, but an endowing graciousness that gives and lets be what is other in its very otherness.

If there is something universal about the agapeic, this universality is an intimate universality. This is something that I think is suggested by the poetic, philosophical, and theological engagements of Michael Martin. The agapeics of the intimate universal goes deep, intensively speaking, and reaches out without restriction, extensively considered. It cannot be confined, and yet it can be most finely attentive to minute particularity and all the nuance of tex-

tured detail. If it is unconfined, it is not merely indefinite or inde-
terminate, but in the language I would choose, it is overdetermined
—more than any finite determination. There is a surplus to determination about it that marks the excess of its generosity, generosity
that cannot be determinately finitized, and that yet is absolutely
homed on the marvel of the finite as finite. It is intimate but not
merely idiosyncratic; it is universal but not merely neutral in a gen-
eralized way. Agape communicates the intimate universally, the universal intimately.

It seems to me that these thoughts gain concrete expression in the
practice of criticism that we find in Michael Martin's book. He
speaks of agapeic criticism—a juxtaposition of terms we do not frequently find within the academic practice of literary criticism.
Among other things fruitfully explored by criticism enlivened by
the generosity of the agapeic are the following: an impossibility of
merely ghettoizing poetic speech; an impossibility of merely cos-
mopolizing more prosaic speech; an impossibility of defining the
poetic as a purely autonomous space of significance that can be
turned back into itself, and be thus self-sufficient for itself; the possibility of essential communication itself as always exceeding the
terms of any form of autonomous self-determination; the possibility, stronger yet, the promise of a fertile porosity between the poetic
and what is often taken to be other to it, most especially religion
and philosophy, as putatively themselves autonomous domains of
significance for themselves. The practice of criticism inspired by the
agapeic opens itself to the promise of this porosity. It is a practice
that is diversely incarnated in the studies that are presented in this
book.

There is something refreshing, in an essential sense, about such a
practice. It restores a promise that is old, it refreshes a possibility
that is still available newly, even when the promise of the agapeic is
not known as such, or perhaps not even suspected. I am thinking
here of the tendency in modernity to define everything in terms of a
culture of autonomy, a culture affecting our understanding of the
poetic also. Sometimes, instead of a great release, we see a retreat
into diverse cells of self-determination: philosophy is to be autonomous, science is to be autonomous, history is to be autonomous,

the arts are to be autonomous. And bringing up the line to make the homogeneity complete, religion, too, is to be autonomous, though this last autonomy is a double-edged sword, since it could be taken as a command to religion just to mind its own business, not to poke its interfering nose into other autonomous domains.

This is a large issue, but it is connected with the weakening of porosity between diverse communications of signification, indeed with the development of bufferings that protect us from exposure to the more terrifying and enlivening transcendences, even in finite life itself. Take this in a certain direction and the result is the closing off of sources of inspiration that cannot be defined in the language of our own self-determination. With Michael Martin we discover the vision beyond such autonomy. We find a worry, indeed dismay, that the poetic might be signing its own death warrant without the influx of communication from the others, and most especially from religious sources of inspiration. *Mutatis mutandis*, the same might be said about these others themselves: the dissipation of philosophical seriousness in the technical scholasticism of analysis or the textual scholasticism of hermeneutics or deconstruction; the slow asphyxiation, indeed desired euthanasia of urgent religious passion, most especially in the enlightened West.

Agapeic criticism, as practiced by Michael Martin, is attentive to all of this. This is continuous with what we have found in his recent book, *The Submerged Reality: Sophiology and the Turn to a Poetic Metaphysics* (Angelico Press, 2015), where sophiology is very much bound up with our mindfulness of the divine *metaxu*. The poetics of Sophia figures importantly in this present book. But Martin also draws attention to different poets whose work witnesses to the signs of the divine *metaxu*. It is not for me to go into the details of these matters here, beyond observing the fact that the poets he singles out for attention, George Herbert and Robert Herrick, are poets who hail from a time when the porous threshold between the poetic and the sacred was granted. Our time finds finesse for this porous threshold sometimes weakened, sometimes not present at all, though sometimes it seems to undergo astonishing resurrections.

Be that as it may, I particularly draw attention to Martin's discussion of poetry and prophecy. This has to do also with the vocation of the critic. He has sharp and wise words to say about the technologization of the calling of the writer. We believe we improve the profession of writing through writing programs, but the results can be the inverse: more professional productions, spiritless writing. We are talking about agapeic criticism, but it is interesting to think of criticism in relation to critique. The word *critique* has been all-pervasive in Western modernity in the last two centuries, experiencing its most famous surge with the three critiques of Immanuel Kant, the first of which opens with the claim that ours is an age of critique, and that nothing should be allowed to escape the bar of judgment where critique reigns. Least of all is religion allowed to escape. Of course, one could say that the cards are stacked in favor of a rationalistic ideal, and when religion plays by the rules of this game, it is preordained always to lose, or at best only to come out as secondary or inferior to reason itself.

But critique is related to the Greek word *krinein*, which also means not only to judge but to discriminate, to discern, to differentiate with finesse. It is this sense of criticism that is most intimately relevant to agapeic criticism. After Kant in philosophy, and generally in humanistic culture, critique takes on the connotation of a certain negative judgment in relation to what culturally precedes us, and again most especially preceding traditions of religion. The latter traditions are viewed through the lenses of autonomy and are more often than not thought to come up short as heteronomous, even tyrannical others that bar autonomy from its more complete and fulfilled self-determination. *Krinein* as *discerning judgment* points us otherwise. If critique is negative critique only, if thinking is understood as a kind of negativity, it is not clear whether through criticism alone anything affirmative can be said. One could well ask here if religion is the most fertile other to obviate such an inward hollowing-out of thinking considered as such a rationally justified negativity. When Martin brings in the prophetic dimension, surely he is reminding us of something very important. Prophetic witness is critical, but it is critical in the name of something that is not merely negative. Prophetic witness is itself open to find itself exposed, not for its own sake, not for its own self-determination, but in the name of another who calls us to communicate to those who are hard of hearing. Agapeic criticism is then prophetic criticism.

There is something of mission about it, just because it is in witness to something other than self. As prophetic, agapeic criticism is indeed vocational, in finding itself called... called by a source of inspiration other than itself, called to communicate this inspiration to those other than itself. We are not the way, we are not the truth, we are not the life. Another companioning power accompanies us on the way—companioning power, like Christ on the road to Emmaus, wonderfully making understandable the Scriptures, making us, the listening fellow-travelers, porous to a communication we do not at first know was, and is, and will be sent by the *incognito* divinity. Only in breaking bread does the Eucharistic awakening come over the disciples that with them along the way and now with them at the table in the inn is the resurrected Christ. They seem to be awake, but being awake they now awake a *second time*, awake beyond the sleeping wakefulness of finite life without God. The prophetic mission of agapeic criticism perhaps awakens us to this second wakefulness. Perhaps such second awakening has something to do with *metanoia*. Perhaps second awakening is what true religion not only promises but delivers, what true philosophizing comes to in its reflective reminders. In *The Incarnation of the Poetic Word* Michael Martin reminds us, through impressive offerings of agapeic reading, that this is what poetry too can do at its best.

WILLIAM DESMOND
Institute of Philosophy,
Katholieke Universiteit Leuven, Belgium
Department of Philosophy,
Villanova University, USA

Introduction

THESE ESSAYS are the product of my thinking over the past twenty or more years concerning poetry and its ontology, an engagement that has led me to questions of both philosophy and theology, often out of a burning necessity. As someone who has followed the simultaneous vocations of poet, philosopher, and theologian, I find that these questions are ever present and, indeed, that they are inseparable to the degree that considering the three of them as distinct domains has come to make little sense to me. The organon has outlived its utility.

The reason these domains seem to have lost their borders for me is the fact that all three vocations are only fully realized through the act of contemplation (and this certainly begs the question whether any vocation participant in contemplation could qualify as poetry, philosophy, or theology—including gardening, beekeeping, music, or carpentry). As John Scotus Eriugena writes, there is something inherently parousaic in the appearing that accompanies the contemplative act:

> *Et notandum est quod theophania potest interpretari quasi ΘΕΟΥ-ΦΑΝΙΑ, hoc est, Dei apparitio vel Dei illuminatio; omne siquidem quod apparet lucet; et a verbo ΦΑΙΝΩ, id est luceo vel appareo, derivatur.*[1]

> [And it should be noted that "theophany" is able to be interpreted as *theo phania*, that is, the appearance of God or the illumination of God; for all that appears shines; and from the verb *phanio*, that is, "I shine" or "I appear" are derived.]

The shining is what interests me here. Just what is it that shines through the poem, the phenomenon, the rite? It is not, as determin-

---

1. John Scotus Eriugena, *Expositiones in Ierarchiam caelestem sancti Dionysii*, IV, 17. The translation is mine.

ism or materialism and their petulant offspring scientism would have us believe, nothing. Our response to it affirms both the appearing and our intuition concerning the source of its illumination. This shining is, as Eriugena notes, theophantic; it is also thoroughly sophianic. And, when it appears, it is inescapable.

But what *is* contemplation? Phenomenology, at least provisionally, has answered this question descriptively, by pointing to the necessity of the epoché as a prerequisite to the phenomenon's disclosure. But phenomenology, at least since Husserl, has erred in attempting to present itself as a "science," *Wissenschaft*. This is not so much a problem of application, as it is a problem of institutionalization: phenomenology has become an "official" discipline with its own turf to defend and alliances to make. Perhaps this was thought necessary in a cultural and academic milieu contending with the real presences of Kant and Descartes? As a result, phenomenology has been over-mystified in the academic world and, in a sense, tragically removed from the worlds with which it claims to be concerned. In truth, it is both easier to understand and more difficult to effect than just about anyone has been willing to admit.

Plotinus may be the most accurate of all philosophers when he defines the contemplative act as a type of play:

> Supposing we played a little before entering upon our serious concern and maintained that all things are striving after Contemplation, looking to Vision as their one end—and this, not merely beings endowed with reason but even the unreasoning animals, the Principle that rules in growing things, and the Earth that produces these—and that all achieve their purpose in the measure possible to their kind, each attaining Vision and possessing itself of the End in its own way and degree, some things in entire reality, others in mimicry and in image—we would scarcely find anyone to endure so strange a thesis. But in a discussion entirely among ourselves there is no risk in a light handling of our own ideas.
>
> Well—in the play of this very moment am I engaged in the act of Contemplation?
>
> Yes; I and all that enter this play are in Contemplation: our play aims at Vision; and there is every reason to believe that child or man, in sport or earnest, is playing or working only towards Vision, that every act is an effort towards Vision; the compulsory

act, which tends rather to bring the Vision down to outward things, and the act thought of as voluntary, less concerned with the outer, originate alike in the effort towards Vision.

The case of Man will be treated later on; let us speak, first, of the earth and of the trees and vegetation in general, asking ourselves what is the nature of Contemplation in them, how we relate to any Contemplative activity the labour and productiveness of the earth, how Nature, held to be devoid of reason and even of conscious representation, can either harbour Contemplation or produce by means of the Contemplation which it does not possess.[2]

For Plotinus, then, contemplation is an activity in which all natural bodies (φύςιν) participate; it is a cosmological reality, a quality of Things. This attentiveness to Things returned to philosophy with phenomenology, albeit in new dress and with new arcana of language. Phenomenological contemplation, then, is both serious play and a playful seriousness. Indeed, prior to the Cartesian revolution scholarly inquiry still retained elements of playfulness, as, for example, in the Renaissance fascination with the *iocus severus*, the serious joke, a commodity now as rare as it is neglected.

So it is with these essays. They represent my playful and serious engagement with their subjects, a metaxological space where the distinctions between philosophy, theology, and poetry are indistinguishable and the beautiful curtain of the world begins to shimmer, if only a little.

---

2. *Enneads* 3.8, 1. Trans. Stephen MacKenna and B.S. Page (New York: Penguin, 1991).

3

Criticism and Contemplation: Steps Toward an Agapaic Criticism

In this chapter, I focus on poetry as the site for exploring a criticism grounded in contemplation and this for a few of reasons. First of all, though a contemplative approach certainly applies to other domains as well, as a scholar of literature and as a poet, as both outside of and within poetry, I feel, despite my inadequacies, a certain obligation to speak on this subject. Secondly, poetry, because of the almost homeo-pathic concentration of language and energy it can possess, aug-mented by its concern with meaning and the disclosure of truth, is the paradigmatic art form for exploring a criticism of contemplation. Human beings to a significant degree associate their being and their selfhood with language. If someone fixes our cars or furnaces, for example, we feel grateful: if they correct our grammar, we feel offended or ashamed. If language is "the house of being," as Heideg-ger claimed (following Hölderlin—a poet), then we should be able to account poetry "the house of the house of being." My long relation-ship with poetry has convinced me, as Jean Wahl has argued, that an honest encounter with poetry reveals poetry by its very nature to be a kind of a spiritual exercise, wherein "Le mystériuex est ici tout près; et l'ici-tout-près est mystériuex"[1] (*"The mysterious is here very near, and the here-very-near is mysterious"*).

IN A LETTER to Fr. Joseph-Marie Perrin written from Marseilles and dated 15 May 1942, the philosopher, activist, and mystic Simone Weil writes of an intimate experience with a poem:

There was a young English Catholic [at Solesmes] from whom I gained my first idea of the supernatural power of the sacraments because of the truly angelic radiance with which he seemed to be clothed after going to communion. Chance—for I always prefer

---

1. Jean Wahl, "La Poésie comme Exercice Spirituel" in *Poésie, Pensée, Perception* (Paris: Calmann-Lévy, 1948), 17–19, at 18.

saying chance rather than Providence—made of him a messenger to me. For he told me of the existence of those English poets of the seventeenth century who are named metaphysical. In reading them later on, I discovered the poem of which I read you what is unfortunately a very inadequate translation. It is called 'Love.' I learned it by heart. Often, at the culminating point of a violent headache, I make myself say it over, concentrating all my attention upon it and clinging with all my soul to the tenderness it enshrines. I used to think I was merely reciting it as a beautiful poem, but without my knowing it the recitation had the virtue of a prayer. It was during one of these recitations that, as I told you, Christ himself came down and took possession of me.[2]

Surely, this is a startling confession, but her experience is not, I think, as rare as one might assume. Weil's encounter with Herbert's poem, though clearly possessing religious significance to her, bears more than a little resonance with what Richard Rorty, hardly a religious thinker, has called an initiatory event of "inspired criticism." For Rorty, inspired criticism originates in the kind of experiences many of us have had: "the result of an encounter with an author, character, plot, stanza, line or archaic torso which has made a difference to the critic's conception of who she is, what she is good for, what she wants to do with herself: an encounter which has rearranged her priorities and purposes."[3] Does anyone study the humanities seriously—certainly at what could be called a "professional level"—without having had such an experience? It is difficult to imagine this not being the case, but, all too often, that initial enthusiasm and astonishment becomes disfigured as sarcasm, suspicion, even contempt, perhaps especially in the case of the "professionals." Weil's intimacy with Herbert's poem, however, challenges such skepticism and puts its adherents on the defensive. Comfortable with a programmatic and doctrinaire naturalism with roots in the Enlightenment, many would dismiss her as deluded, regressed, clinging to infantile fantasies, narcissistic, or worse. Even in her

2. Simone Weil, *Waiting for God*, trans. Emma Craufurd (1951; reprt., New York: Harper Perennial, 2009), 26–27.
3. Richard Rorty, *Philosophy and Social Hope* (London: Penguin, 1999), 145.

sensitive, sympathetic documentary, *An Encounter with Simone Weil*, director Julia Haslett describes her subject's religious turn as "a betrayal." Why a betrayal? The answer is obvious. But, I think, it is rather a question of how some, holding to the outdated and insufficient assumptions of materialistic and scientistic triumphalism, have betrayed Weil and what she represents. Indeed, she demands that we consider the relationship of transcendence and immanence, two words that serve as more-or-less socially acceptable substitutes for what Henri de Lubac calls "surnaturel."[4] Understood from this perspective, we can start to understand how Weil's experience reaches even deeper into the nature of the human person than the issues of identity and aesthetics upon which Rorty touches. In experiences like Weil's, the artifact, the poem in her case, occupies a curious role: simultaneously the source of the experience and, paradoxically, even mysteriously, that through which the experience arrives. Indeed, as in the case in a work of stained glass, the poem is incomplete, inert, as it were, without a source of illumination.

A central feature of Weil's experience and those to which Rorty points is that they arise out of a contemplative engagement with a work. First of all, Weil translated the poem and then furthered her intimacy with it by committing it to memory, learning it *by heart*, to use a very apt metaphor. Translation is an incredibly intimate act and bears distinctly religious/spiritual, even supernatural overtones (think: Bottom's translation in *A Midsummer Night's Dream*, for instance, or, in a very different register the translations of Elijah and Enoch). Indeed, we might say that not only did Weil translate the poem, but the poem, in fact, translated her, utterly transfiguring her through the encounter with it.

The dwelling with the artifact; our presence to it; our acceptance of it, as it is, in itself: this is contemplation. Chrétien de Troyes, in *Le*

---

4. Most significantly in Henri de Lubac, *Surnaturel: Études Historiques* (Paris: Aubier, 1946). See also John Milbank's examination of de Lubac's theology, *The Suspended Middle: Henri de Lubac and the Debate concerning the Supernatural* (Grand Rapids, MI: William B. Eerdmans, 2005).

Conte du Graal provides a wonderful illustration of one of the onto-logical effects (or perhaps prerequisites) of dwelling in contempla-tion. As the young knight Perceval falls into reverie at the sight of three drops of blood on the snow (an image which reminds him of the complexion of his beloved), the poet tells us "Si pense tant que il s'oblie"—he thinks until he himself is forgotten.[5] Weil, in abiding with the poem and absenting herself from the obligations of analy-sis—not to mention suffering from a migraine—in a very real sense "thinks until she herself is forgotten" which allows the event to take place. This forgetfulness of self, a form of phenomenological reduc-tion, is essential to the criticism of contemplation.

In his philosophico-scientific poesis, contemplation was so important to Goethe that he dared assert that "Every object, well contemplated, opens a new organ of perception in us."[6] Goethe's insight has inspired physicist Arthur Zajonc to such a degree that the latter encourages a method he calls *contemplative inquiry*, a way of scholarship be believes aids analytical modalities through what he calls "an epistemology of love," asserting that such an epistemol-ogy is "the true heart of higher education."[7] I like this idea very much. However, Zajonc's ethos seems antithetical to most contem-porary pedagogical and critical approaches we find in the humani-ties; approaches, alas, generally indifferent if not hostile to the very notion of such an epistemology.

The term "contemplation," of course, possesses both religious and scholarly inflections and, I admit, it is not always easy to distin-guish between the two. For example, "Contemplation," according to one definition, "signifies a clear, ready, mental seeing and quiet regarding of an object, being the result and effect of a precedent

---

5. Chrétien de Troyes, *Le Roman de Perceval, ou Le Conte du Graal*, ed. William Roach (Genève: Librarie Droz, 1959), line 4202.

6. Johann Wolfgang von Goethe, *Scientific Studies: The Collected Works*, vol. 12 (Princeton: Princeton University Press, 1995), 39.

7. Arthur Zajonc, "Attending to Interconnection, Living the Lesson" in *The Heart of Higher Education: A Call to Renewal. Transforming the Academy through Collegial Conversations* by Parker J. Palmer and Arthur Zajonc, with Megan Scrib-ner (San Francisco: Josey-Bass, 2010), 77–100, at 94.

diligent and laborious inquiry and search after the nature, qualities, dependencies, and other circumstantial conditions of it."[8] This seems rather prosaic and academic—yet it comes from an important early modern work on the contemplative religious life, Dom Augustine Baker's *Sancta Sophia* (1662). Baker's definition also anticipates the methods of phenomenology.

Phenomenology, of course, is a discipline familiar with what William Desmond might call the metaxological space between philosophy and theology (or even mysticism), though such a blurring of distinctions is not without its critics. Dominique Janicaud, for instance, himself working out of phenomenology, called into question phenomenologist Jean-Luc Marion and what has been called the "theological turn" in French phenomenology.[9] But a religious turn, it seems, is somewhat implicit to phenomenology and was clearly not unknown during phenomenology's German nascence. Max Scheler, Edith Stein, Adolf Reinach, Hedwig Conrad-Martius, Dietrich von Hildebrand, and, one could say, both Karol Wojtyla and Rudolf Steiner all experienced religious or spiritual awakenings due to their phenomenological investigations.[10] As Angela Ales Bello has recently argued, Edmund Husserl's phenomenological project, from its inception, inhabited a space inherently mindful of the question of God.[11] Husserl, in fact, ends his *Cartesian Meditations* in words, including a quotation from St. Augustine, that clearly evoke religious sensibilities and the ethos of contemplation: "Positive science is lost in the world. I must lose the world by epoché, in order to regain it by a universal self-examination. '*Noli foras ire,*' says

8. Dom Augustine Baker, *Holy Wisdom [Sancta Sophia] or Directions for the Prayer of Contemplation, Extracted out of more than Forty Treatises*, digested by R. F. Serenus Cressy, ed. Abbot Sweeney (New York: Harper & Brothers, 1950), 4.1.2 (502–03).

9. See, in particular, Dominique Janicaud, *Phenomenology "Wide Open": After the French Debate*, trans. Charles N. Cabral (New York: Fordham University Press, 2005).

10. I am surprised that, to date, no one has undertaken a study of this phenomenon.

11. Angela Ales Bello, *The Divine in Husserl and Other Explorations*, trans. Anthony Calcagno, *Analecta Husserliana 98*, ed. Anna-Teresa Tyminiecka (Dordrecht: Springer, 2012).

Augustine, '*in te redi, in interiore homine habitat veritas.*'[12] (Do not go out, but return into yourself. In the inner man dwells truth.) Scholars routinely label Heidegger a mystic: sometimes in the way of an epithet, sometimes in the way of praise. Similar charges have been levied against Emmanuel Levinas and Jacques Derrida.

Husserl famously described phenomenology, with its dedication to returning "to the things themselves," as "first philosophy."[13] My contention is that phenomenology is also "first criticism." I find it perplexing to see so many colleagues in my discipline take first recourse in criticism to turn to the almost tribal reflexes of their chosen critical allegiances, which eventually become hermeneutical cages. Such moves cannot by any claims be construed as "first criticism," but as second or third at best. William Desmond, following Ricouer, has called such critical gestures "a hermeneutics of suspicion,"[14] recalling Harold Bloom's more indecorous and infamous label, "Schools of Resentment."[15] One wonders how much such negative hermeneutics have contributed to the decline of the influence of the humanities both in academic culture ánd, more importantly, in the culture at large. It cannot be negligible. And this critical stance is not only characteristic of scholarship in the humanities.

The twentieth-century theologian Hans Urs von Balthasar, himself no stranger to phenomenology, observes that, in biblical studies, hermeneutics and other secondary interpretive technologies have usurped the primacy of the contemplation of the object itself. "Does it not make one suspicious," he writes, "when Biblical philology's first move in its search for an 'understanding' of its texts is to dissect their form into sources, psychological motivations, and the

---

12. Edmund Husserl, *Cartesian Meditations: An Introduction to Phenomenology*, trans. Dorion Cairns (The Hague: Martinus Nijhoff, 1960), 157.

13. Edmund Husserl, *Ideas Pertaining to a Pure Phenomenology and to a Phenomenological Philosophy, First Book: General Introduction to a Pure Phenomenology*, trans. F. Kersten (The Hague: Springer, 1982), §19 (page 35), §63 (page 148).

14. William Desmond, *The Intimate Strangeness of Being: Metaphysics after Dialectic* (Washington, DC: The Catholic University of America Press, 2012), 26.

15. Harold Bloom, Preface to *The Anxiety of Influence: A Theory of Poetry*, 2nd ed. (New York: Oxford University Press, 1997), xv.

sociological effects of the milieu, even before the form has been really contemplated and read for its meaning *as form*?"[16] I am suspicious, I confess, of critical enterprises in literary studies that turn first to the institutionalized biases of their own discourses and place the text in question into predetermined categories. Is it possible that we are all guilty, at times, of the "enormous condescension of posterity"?[17] This is not to say that studies which seek sources, psychological motivations, sociological pressures, and other contexts are invalid interpretive modes. Clearly, they may hold value in themselves and, as Maurice Merleau-Ponty has observed, for phenomenological studies, "[t]he other's gaze on things is a second openness."[18] But they are removed from the things themselves and, like a photocopy of a photocopy of a photocopy of an original document, significantly distanced from the originary artifact. Indeed, theory's tendency is to interpret the artifact in terms of the critic.

Interestingly, perhaps ironically, the Greek word for contemplation is *theoria* ($\theta\varepsilon o\rho\acute{\iota}\alpha$). Theory, however, as it is now understood in literary criticism, is not very recognizable as contemplation. Rather, it is an *organon* ($\H{o}\rho\gamma\alpha\nu o\nu$), a tool, an instrument for arranging concepts and ideas. It may be utilitarian, pragmatic, even political, but it is not at all organic. Such a mechanistic approach to literary criticism, unmitigated by something more "living," I think, runs the danger of becoming somewhat damaging and, ultimately, deadening. It hollows out and trivializes the immediate experience of the phenomenon, of literature, an experience that once (or more) drew so many of us into a state of astonishment, and runs the risk of killing it through vivisection. In examining the historical arc of philosophy, Nikolai Berdyaev has observed that "While in official phi-

---

16. Hans Urs von Balthasar, *The Glory of the Lord: A Theological Aesthetics, Volume I: Seeing the Form*, ed. Joseph Fessio, S.J. and John Riches, trans. Erasmo Leiva-Merikakis (San Francisco: Ignatius, 1982), 31. Balthasar's emphasis.

17. E.P. Thompson, *The Making of the English Working Class* (1963; reprt. Harmondsworth: Penguin, 1986), 12.

18. Maurice Merleau-Ponty, *The Visible and the Invisible, followed by Working Notes*, ed. Claude Lefort, trans. Alphonso Lingis (Evanston, IL: Northwestern University Press, 1968), 59.

losophy, from Descartes on, the mechanistic conception of nature triumphed and, with rare exceptions, philosophy could not overcome the spectre of a dead mechanism of nature, for mystic philosophy nature always remained something alive, a living organism."[19] Like Berdyaev's "mystic philosophy," a criticism grounded in phenomenology, what I would like to call (with a nod to Desmond) *agapeic criticism*, allows us to view the literary artifact not as a dead mechanism of history/subjectivity but, indeed, as "something alive, a living organism." Agapeic criticism as method attends to the poem as a "living artifact" (oxymoron intended) which contains access to being, the being of the poem as well as the being of the poet, not to mention, in the most remarkable of cases, the being of the absolutely Other. In the contemplative presence to a poem characteristic of agapeic criticism, the poem becomes one's environment. One truly "enters into" the poem, abiding with presence(s) informing the poem.

The power of a phenomenological approach to literature, "texts" as we call them, resides in the epoché, the bracketing of preconceptions and assumptions in order to invite a purer experience of the phenomenon standing before one. A text—etymologically, poetically, literally—is "something woven." It possesses its own texture, context, subtext, perhaps pretext. The epoché allows one to be present to the text, to dwell with it. This is the importance of Weil's experience with Herbert's "Love": she lived with this poem, moving beyond analysis and dialectic and opening herself to the poem itself quite naturally but in the way one might cultivate a garden—in patient waiting, acceptance, abiding attention. What she did not do was bother herself with trying to "understand" the poem or categorize it according to a predetermined critical apparatus. The epoché allows our abiding, but the epoché is not easy. This is especially the case in our often contentious times and milieu which seem almost to require an agenda when encountering a text, an obsession with commentary fairly democratized and rendered absurd if not inert in the culture of commentary on internet news sites and social media.

---

19. Nicolas Berdyaev, *The Meaning of the Creative Act*, trans. Donald A. Lowrie (New York: Collier Books, 1962), 68.

But the epoché is not without danger. A phenomenological reading of a text is an experience of intimacy and, like all forms of intimacy, both subject and object expose themselves to vulnerability. This can be uncomfortable. Indeed, a phenomenological attention to reading can divulge a somewhat disturbing—but possibly also inspiring—level of awareness. As Georges Poulet has argued, in reading,

> I am aware of a rational being, of a consciousness; the consciousness of another, no different from the one I automatically assume in every human being I encounter, except in this case the consciousness is open to me, welcomes me, lets me look deep inside itself, and even allows me, with unheard-of licence, to think what it thinks and feel what it feels. . . . Because of the strange invasion of my person by the thoughts of another, I am a self who is granted the experience of thinking thoughts foreign to him. I am the subject of thoughts other than my own. My consciousness behaves as though it were the consciousness of another.[20]

Such an experience could be a little disquieting—or, on the other hand, enlivening—but, in general, it is not. Why not? It should be, at least some of the time. Perhaps what Poulet also discloses here, indirectly, is our inherent inattentiveness or laziness in the act of reading. Perhaps a fear of intimacy explains why an initial response to an unfamiliar text is often one of resistance.

We struggle with the text, and with the author, agonistically, in our encounters with them. We, in a very real sense, *contend* with them. This may be why, when one learns a poem "by heart" or approaches it agapeically that it slowly opens, like a flower, of its own accord but attentive to "atmospheric conditions"—time, place, state-of-soul, and so on—as happened in the case of Weil. Through this relationship we build with the poem, we eventually "come to know it" in a way not unlike Adam "knew" Eve: intimately, but more than bodily or intellectually. It moves from the spirit level and opens into the soul, and from there affects the physical, carnality, the flesh. John Panteleimon Manoussakis notices a similar phenomenon in the discomfort one can feel when praying before an icon: a

20. Georges Poulet, "The Phenomenology of Reading," *New Literary History* 1 no. 1 (1969): 53–68, at 54 and 56.

sudden realization that, while one gazes at an icon, one is also seen from beyond the image.[21] Manoussakis calls this *inverse intentionality*, "a chiastic point where the two extremes cross paths,"[22] though I prefer the term *double intentionality*, as the phenomenon is given as a very real meeting of two centers of consciousness. Marion and Levinas entertain this notion in the context of the confrontation with the other; what Manoussakis (and I) consider, though, is how the intentionality of the other is encountered archeologically, one might say, through our intentional presence to the artifact. There may be, I acknowledge, other ways to *explain* the phenomenon, but this is an accurate description of the eventamental character of the experience itself.

It might be argued that the agapeic critical gesture is merely *lectio divina* masquerading as philosophy, but this is not the case. *Lectio divina*, indeed, may sometimes result in the experience of astonishment common to phenomenological readings—seeing that *lectio divina* is oriented to "science and knowledge" by theologians and "wisdom and appreciation" for contemplatives[23]—but *lectio divina* is just as predetermined (though perhaps more generous of spirit) than critical gestures arising out of theory. *Lectio divina*, that is, like theory-driven readings, does not hold to the epoché. Entering into an encounter with a text, a phenomenon, without a goal in mind is what opens the possibility for the epoché to result in an experience of astonishment. And this astonishment occurs when we encounter truth—for what is more astonishing than truth? The epoché, then, becomes an agapeic opening to the truth behind, buried within, and abiding with the phenomenon; or, in Heidegger's words, "the clearing and concealing of what is."[24] Such an openness clearly informed

---

21. John P. Manoussakis, "The Phenomenon of God: From Husserl to Marion," *American Catholic Philosophical Quarterly* 78, no. 1 (2004): 53–68, at 64.

22. Ibid., 62.

23. Jean Leclerq, *The Love of Learning and the Desire for God: A Study of Monastic Culture*, trans. Catharine Misrahi (New York: Fordham University Press, 1961), 89.

24. Martin Heidegger, "The Origin of the Work of Art" in *Poetry, Language, Thought*, trans. Albert Hofstadter (New York: Harper & Row Publishers, 1971), 72.

Edith Stein's approach to reading, particularly her encounter with St. Teresa of Avila's autobiography, a book she read in one sitting and which compelled her upon completing it to acknowledge, "This is the truth."[25] Such a disclosure of truth witnesses to the poetic, to poesis: an encounter with the maker, a moment of ἀναγνώρισις, recognition. As Stein's colleague Heidegger observes, "All art, as the letting happen of the advent of the truth of what is, is, as such, *essentially poetry*."[26] Of course, not all art is art and not all poetry is poetry. We know this. This complicates things. The kind of art I am considering is that which, as Stein writes, "mysteriously suggests the whole fullness of meaning, for which all human knowledge is inexhaustible. Understood in this way, all genuine art is revelation and all artistic creation is sacred service."[27] Only an agapeic reading can affirm a poem's access to being.

The encounter with a work which "mysteriously suggests the whole fullness of meaning" is an event that deserves serious consideration, but usually does not receive it in theory or literary studies. In the case of poetry, which Heidegger rightly intuited as that which has the potential to "[convert] that nature of ours which merely wills to impose, together with its objects, into the innermost invisible region of the heart's space,"[28] I would like to examine how a poem might open through an agapeic approach.

In reading a poem, first of all, we are confronted, as Poulet has said, with the consciousness of another. In an agapeic encounter with the poem, we dwell empathetically with it, bracketing our assumptions about historicity, politics, even gender—bracketing them, but not forever erasing them. In Bello's words, "Through the lived experience of empathy my consciousness goes beyond itself and discovers another consciousness, but through this other consciousness one can delineate the psychic and spiritual life of the

---

25. Kieran Kavanaugh, O.C.D., Introduction to *The Science of the Cross* by Edith Stein, *The Collected Works of Edith Stein*, vol. 6, trans. Josephine Koeppel (Washington, DC: ICS Publications, 2002), xiv.

26. Heidegger, "Origin of the Work of Art," 72. Emphasis in Heidegger.

27. Edith Stein, *Science of the Cross*, 12.

28. Heidegger, "What Are Poets for?" *Poetry, Language, Thought*, 72.

other, who places himself or herself in relation to others through consciousness."[29] Who has not undertaken a serious study of an author and not thought that he or she really knows the author in question? Indeed, do we not say, when engaged with a study of their works, that we are reading Herbert, for instance, or Blake, or Eliot—reading, that is, *them*. This intuition arises from empathy. This empathy, however, reminds us that the critical act—any critical act—can never be entirely, perhaps even remotely, objective. It is analogous to our participation as auditors to an inspired performance: we recognize something profound and we are ourselves part of the profundity—and we don't need to consult the Heisenberg principle to know this to be the case. The Spanish poet Federico Garcia Lorca describes this participatory ecstasy in terms of the *Duende*, a "mysterious power that all may feel and no philosophy can explain"[30] which he believes to be potential in all art forms, but finds most commonly in music, dance, and spoken poetry.[31] Lorca defines such an inspired experience as "profound, human, tender, the cry of communion with God through the medium of the five senses and the grace of the *Duende*," ultimately enacting "the unending baptism of all newly-created things."[32] Herbert's poem "Love," indeed, became a new creation through Weil's contemplation of it. She gained access to the originary creative act of the poem, reaching its being, reaching the being of Herbert's poetic performance, and touching, she claimed, even the Being of Christ. But, even as Being is disclosed in an agapeic reading, it is not exhausted. Much is still hidden, or else Weil would not be able to associate it with divinity. It possesses more of theophany than of revelation (though that is present as well): it is something to be experienced rather than comprehended. The amount of truth made available through an open presence to a poem's Saying, in Heidegger's words, "sets all present beings free into their given presence,

---

29. Bello, *Divine in Husserl*, 34.

30. Lorca quotes Goethe's response to a performance by violinist Niccolo Paganini. Federico Garcia Lorca, "The *Duende*: Theory and Divertissement," in *Poet in New York*, trans. Ben Belitt (New York: Grove Press, 1955), 154.

31. Ibid., 159.

32. Ibid., 158–59; 166.

and brings what is absent into their absence."[33] In an agapeic reading of poetry, the wholly unspoken may indeed shine through the text as the holy unspoken.

Through a phenomenological reduction, the poem (though, surely, not every poem) can become what Marion calls a "saturated phenomenon," that which "saturate[s] intuition to such an extent that all horizons are shattered."[34] The poem presents itself to me: it is printed on a page; it appears, hopefully, in a language I know; it was written at some time by someone for some reason. The poem also discloses meanings, both explicit and implicit. But the phenomenon of the poem does not show everything—and my intuition still apprehends something other. Marion, using Husserl's famous example of a tobacco box, reminds us that when we examine the box our intuition fills in that which we do not see (the side of the box beyond our seeing, for example) an experience which "already conceals and reveals an invisibility" which, following Husserl, he calls a "phenomenology of the unapparent."[35] The invisible, the unapparent that arrives in the contemplation of a poem, contributes significantly to the "saturatedness" of the poem. Invoking his concept of the icon, Marion (in language Manoussakis will appropriate), though speaking of the icon of the face, aptly describes the iconographic function of poetry as well:

> What I see of them, if I see anything of them that *is*, does not result from the constitution I would assign to them in the visible, but from the effect they produce on me. And, in fact, this happens in reverse so that my look is submerged, in a counter-intentional manner. Then I am no longer the transcendental *I* but rather the witness, constituted by what happens to him or her. Hence the para-dox, inverted *doxa*. In this way, the phenomenon that befalls and happens to us reverses the order of visibility in that it no

33. Martin Heidegger, "The Way to Language," in *On the Way to Language*, trans. Peter D. Hertz (New York: Harper Collins, 1971), 126.

34. Robyn Horner and Vincent Berraud, Translator's Introduction to *In Excess: Studies of Saturated Phenomena* by Jean-Luc Marion (New York: Fordham University Press, 2001), ix.

35. Jean-Luc Marion, *In Excess*, 105 and 109.

longer results from my intention but from its own counter-intentionality.[36]

The Greek word *paradoxos* (παράδοξος), etymologically, means "counter opinion" or, better, "beyond opinion," "alongside opinion." But *doxos* (δοξος) also means "glory"—and here I mean glory in a religious sense. The inverted *doxa* (δοξος), disclosed by the epoché, then, not only astonishes by means of a phenomenality that exceeds opinion; it also astonishes as an inverted glory, a glory turned back and refracted through the poem.

And so we come to the question of God.

It is not my intention in this chapter to prove the existence of God by way of poetry. Perhaps we are not ready in this investigation to begin naming names. Nevertheless, Benjamin's hunchback continues to haunt us.[37] But we do need to start thinking about what exactly it is that occasionally shines through the poem in an agapeic reading. We feel it, are moved by it, participate in it, so it is not "nothing." Balthasar calls this shining quality "splendour," a phenomenon which "brings with it a self-evidence that en-lightens without mediation."[38] Considering the effects of transcendent beauty becoming immanent (a very real *translatio*), Balthasar contemplates the phenomenon as process:

> The form as it appears to us is beautiful only because the delight that it arouses in us is founded upon the fact that, in it, the truth and goodness of the depths of reality itself are manifested and bestowed, and this manifestation and bestowal reveal themselves to us as being something infinitely and inexhaustibly valuable and fascinating. The appearance of the form, as revelation of the depths, is an indissoluble union of two things. It is the real presence of the depths, of the whole of reality, *and* it is a real pointing beyond itself to these depths. . . . We 'behold' the form; but, if we really behold it, it is not as a detached form, rather in its unity

36. Ibid., 113.

37. Walter Benjamin, "Theses on the Philosophy of History" in *Illuminations*, edited with an introduction by Hannah Arendt, trans. by Harry Zohn (New York: Schocken Books, 1968), 253–64, at 253.

38. Balthasar, *Glory of the Lord: A Theological Aesthetics, Volume I: Seeing the Form*, 37.

with the depths that make their appearance in it. We see form as splendour, as the glory of Being.[39]

The glory of Being the theologian Balthasar speaks of here has more than a little in common with the philosopher Heidegger's assertion that "The art work opens up in its own way the Being of beings,"[40] a statement we could also read as the "Being behind beings." While it is true that Heidegger typically proves rather cagey when it comes to the question of God (a trait also evident in Derrida), there can be no mistaking the metaphysical and onto-theological implications of this statement. Weil, both a philosopher and a mystic, moves beyond the theoretical commitments and responsibilities of theology and philosophy and, unashamedly and unflinchingly, touches the mystery itself. Her experience is not unique, not even unique to readers of poetry. Heidegger's engagement with Rilke and Hölderlin among other poets certainly testifies to this, as do the undocumented experiences of uncounted numbers of sensitive, attentive readers. Others may not have a platform similar to Weil's and Heidegger's from which to share their experiences, they may lack the vocabulary or conceptual framework to put these experiences into context, or, sadly, they may fear exposing themselves to scandal and ridicule. Some may lack the ability or desire to put their experiences into language. But Wahl speaks truth when he speaks of poetry as a kind of spiritual exercise. An agapeic reading of poetry may become just this. Theories about religious experiences abound, but it is a good idea to bear in mind, as Heidegger advised, that "religious experiences are not theoretical."[41] Nor are the experiences of Being attained through an agapeic reading of poetry.

---

39. Ibid., 118–19. Balthasar's emphasis.
40. Heidegger, "Origin of the Work of Art," 39.
41. Martin Heidegger, *The Phenomenology of Religious Life*, Studies in Continental Thought, trans. Matthias Fritsch and Jennifer Anna Gosetti-Ferencei (Bloomington, IN: Indiana University Press, 2010), 236.

What is Phenomenology For?

I

"Becoming more and more logical, one takes to writing commentaries on works of art. This is a terrible product of a materialistic age: scholars write commentaries on art. But these academic explanations, Faust *commentaries,* Hamlet *commentaries, learned descriptions of the art of Leonardo, Raphael, Michelangelo, are coffins in which genuine artistic feeling, living art, lie buried. If one picks up a* Faust *or* Hamlet *commentary, it is like touching a corpse. Abstract thoughts have murdered the work of art."*

RUDOLF STEINER, 18 May 1923[1]

WORKS OF literary criticism, all too often, attempt to instruct us about the living by means of the dead, treating works of genius as if they were formaldehyded frogs. And by "the dead" I do not mean to imply the historiography or philology with which Steiner would have been familiar, though those methods of excavation and their inheritors certainly incline toward the tomb. What I have in mind in particular are the modes of literary criticism which proliferate in our own age—of Marxist, feminist, queer, psychoanalytic, and New Historicist critical gestures and so forth which tend to take the text in question not on its own terms but, rather, on their own. While such critical modes can at times yield valuable insights about cultures and our own age, they tell us precious little about how to read works of art in their primacy as expressions of being. Only phenomenology can do that.

---

1. Rudolf Steiner, *The Arts and Their Mission*, trans. Lisa D. Monges and Virginia Moore (Spring Valley, NY: The Anthroposophic Press, 1964), 85.

II

The dead. In the work of art, the poem for example, we are not faced with an artifact; we are not faced with the traces of the dead. No. Under the proper conditions, we pass into the life signified by the phenomenon. Life is not found in death. We cannot be enlivened by the dead. We already know this.

III

Most critical modes engage a phenomenon, a text or work of art, for example, without first having listened to its own singular utterance. What the work has to say is of very little consequence in the presence of what the critic wishes to say. In this way, at the very least, these modes of inquiry lack both humility and charity wherein the most obvious question never comes into question. Can a work of art tell us anything unless we listen to it?

IV

Approaching a work of art with a political axe to grind is what William Desmond has called a "betrayal of reverence." Approaching a text without the possibility of reverence, without an openness to the possible, absolutely poisons the relationship between reader and text, beholder and the beheld, even before it begins. Without reverence, the human being "turns into a monster."[2] A reader or critic's lack of reverence renders everything he or she beholds as likewise monstrous. Our disposition of soul colors all we see. *Ubi caritas.*

V

Phenomenology, or (to be more precise) working phenomenologically, is not easily defined. This is because phenomenology, ultimately, is not an apparatus one applies to phenomena, not a tool or application. Rather, it is a way of being, or, to use Heidegger's language, a way of dwelling poetically. For Heidegger, indeed, "the

---

2. William Desmond, *Is There a Sabbath for Thought?* Perspectives in Continental Philosophy (New York: Fordham University Press, 2005), 263.

poetic is the basic capacity for human dwelling."[3] It is the integral human gesture. And we have forgotten how to do it. Our disposition of soul colors all we see. If we dwell in the monstrous, we see monsters. If we dwell in the poetic, in being, we see being. Or rather, being is disclosed to us through the poetic. Thus mysterion.

VI

The mysterion prefers to present itself in deceptive simplicity. As complement to this simplicity, in resonance to it, the mysterion most properly arises in the presence of *humility*. An attitude of reverence, standing before the phenomenon without judgment. Humility occasions the unfolding of the phenomenon before which one stands. Such reverence is not a form of religious worship or piety, but something more in the way of respect or honor. The mood, to hazard a religious image, is pentecostal. That is, in the epoché, we stand before the phenomenon in attentive patience, awaiting its self-disclosure. The self-disclosure, then—strangely, it must be admitted—manifests in the arrival of the unseen.

VII

The invisible starts to shine through the visible when the beholder's self-awareness begins to vanish—if only momentarily—at the horizon of beholding. A true reciprocal relationship. Heidegger, acutely aware of the presence of the absent in acts of language (particularly in poetry), reflects on this, writing,

> It is what brings all present and absent beings each into their own, from where they show themselves in what they are, and where they abide according to their kind. . . . It yields the opening of the clearing in which present beings persist and from which absent beings can depart while keeping their persistence in withdrawal.[4]

Is Heidegger's utterance metaphor? I do not think it is. The absent

3. Martin Heidegger, *Poetry, Language, Thought,* trans. Albert Hofstadter (New York: Harper & Row Publishers, 1971), 228.

4. Martin Heidegger, *On the Way to Language,* trans. Peter D. Hertz (New York: Harper & Row, 1971), 127.

(the poet in the case of a poem) shows himself through the poem while the present (the reader) witnesses—and, indeed, is the vessel of, participates in—the clearing. This is presence, *parousia*, mysterion.

VIII

What do we meet through the poem as-it-is, the poem written from being and not from persona? We meet being. We meet an Other. This is a purely spiritual experience occasioned by the physicality of paper and ink. Paper and ink become the magic circle within which the angel appears. So much danger. Though filled with beauty, as Maritain reminded us, not every angel wishes us well.

IX

There are varying degrees of the poetic-phenomenological encounter. Poetry anchored in the persona is clouded by distortion: clever, perhaps, but ultimately impenetrable to intentionality. Poetry anchored in the poet's being, on the other hand, responds to intentionality, disclosing the poet's own intentionality. An opportunity for communion. Some religious poetry—Herbert, Traherne, Vaughan, Milosz, Eliot, Gascoyne—strives for the Being beyond being. This opens the potential for another horizon's disclosure.

X

Who is the creator in a work disdaining creation?
Charles Taylor identifies the splendor of the poetic—particularly (though not exclusively) in the Romantics—as that "which brings us into the presence of something which is otherwise inaccessible, and which is of the highest moral or spiritual significance; a manifestation, moreover, which also defines or completes something, even as it reveals."[5] A fair description of *parousia*. He is aware that modernist (and postmodernist) artistic epiphanies tend to reject this possibility, that they reject the world and being; that they look to the work as its own splendor, a feedback loop joying in the beauty of

5. Charles Taylor, *Sources of the Self: The Making of Modern Identity* (Cambridge: Harvard University Press, 1989), 419.

distortion, the impossibility of the good, and the transgressivity of a truthless truth. But is it not really the case that works of art closed from presence, closed from the possibility of *parousia*, are open to another kind of presence, albeit similarly disregarded and (absolutely) unintended? Presence may not be welcome—yet there is still a presence. The Evil One is called *simius Dei* because he cannot create. But he appears a glorified figure.

XI

"And thus we have come to believe that it is through reverie that one must learn phenomenology."

Gaston Bachelard[6]

Reverie is a wakeful abidingness forgetful of self, an absolute presence to the phenomenon. This is a paradox. We do it all the time. Phenomenology may be first philosophy. It is also first criticism, first attention to presence.

XII

Humility, generosity, acceptance . . . these are implicit to phenomenological presence. Are they antecedent to it, or consequences of it?

XIII

Nietzsche, writing in 1873: "The weakness of modern personality comes out well in the measureless overflow of criticism, in the want of self-mastery, and in what the Romans called *impotentia*."[7] The power exerted by the critic is a power that is not power—like that Creon wields over Antigone. Lack of self-mastery leads to the desire to master others, ends in impotence, the physiological manifestation of a psychological malady. Ours is the Age of Hostility: towards fertility, towards nature, towards poetry, towards the sublime, towards

---

6. Gaston Bachelard, *The Poetics of Reverie: Childhood, Language, and the Cosmos*, trans. Daniel Russell (Boston: Beacon Press, 1969), 14.

7. Friedrich Nietzsche, *The Use and Abuse of History*, trans. Adrian Collins (Indianapolis, IN: Library of Liberal Arts, 1949), 34.

parousia, towards anything other. Sterility's hidden sovereignty: the desire for stasis.

XIV

The mysterion of the "I." For Emil Staiger, no distance exists between the poem and the listener, or between the poet and his subject. "The lyric poet usually says 'I,'" Staiger writes. "But he says it differently than does the author of an autobiography."[8] For Georges Poulet the "I" becomes the point of contact for a strange type of intimacy: "Whenever I read, I mentally pronounce an *I*, and yet the *I* which I pronounce is not myself.... Another *I*, who has replaced my own and who will continue to do so as long as I read."[9] What is this "I" that is not I? A lure drawing psychological immanence into transcendence and transcendence into immanence? This is possible. A simple case of the "willing suspension of disbelief"? This is an excuse. What we discover is a willing (though often un- or only semi-conscious) intentionality of trust. We allow the other into our souls, place our souls within the other. The movement is reciprocal. What is the condition of one's "I" in the act of reading?

XV

Husserl's mistake: calling phenomenology a science, a behavioral tic he carried over from Brentano. Is this also attributable to an attempted rehabilitation of Descartes on Husserl's part? A way to legitimize the epoché by grounding it in the *cogito*? Is it a demand for respect from the academic powers, an attempt to preserve the human subject from the dehumanizing forces of an unchecked rationality while simultaneously pitching a tent in the enemy's camp? Husserl's age suffered from a kind of penis envy with the sciences as the boy and the humanities as the jealous girl. Freud was wrong, of course. And, at least here, so was Husserl.

---

8. Emil Staiger, *Basic Concepts of Poetics* (*Grundbegriffe der Poetik*), trans. Janette C. Hudson and Luanne T. Frank, ed. Marianne Burkhard and Luanne T. Frank (University Park, PA: The Pennsylvania University Press, 1991), 76.

9. Georges Poulet, "The Phenomenology of Reading," *New Literary History*, 1 no. 1 (October 1969): 53–68, at 56–7.

XVI

Phenomenology may be a kind of *episteme,* a *scientia,* a way of knowing. But it is a way of knowing foreign to the knowing characterized by acquisitiveness and the desire to possess, the psychological correlate of "the claim." Phenomenology refuses the temptation to colonize the phenomenon. This is a temptation that post-colonial criticism has yet to resist.

XVII

Some may argue that Husserl's *Wissenschaft* is not the same thing as what we think of in English as "science." His admiration of Descartes argues otherwise. Steiner (who also studied under Brentano) committed the same mistake by naming his work *Geisteswissenschaft,* "spiritual science." Both Husserl and Steiner were engaged in a similar project: the scientific apprehension of the invisible through revolutionary and subjective modes of investigation. In this they strayed from a pure phenomenology.

XVIII

The uses of mysterion. Parousia.
Epoché prepares the way for presence. First, the subject's own presence to the phenomenon. This is followed by the experience of the opening, the unfolding of the phenomenon, a kind of shimmering. Then the disclosure of the phenomenon, both visible and invisible. Presence meets presence, enters into presence, discloses a previously hidden horizon. Patient repose occupies both the time and the space between presences. The gospel example of this is John the Baptist. His epoché dwelt in preparation, and his patience was not troubled by the desire for proof. The parousaic disclosure in the Jordan.

XIX

The application of "scholarship" often interferes with the disclosure of phenomena. The scholarship of theology, the scholarship of philosophy, just as with the scholarship of literature, are often *about* their subjects but do not enter *into* them. There is something gossipy and tensile about such gestures, something redolent of the egregore. The sense of security found in the communion of the egregore assures the endeavor will never *become* theology or philosophy but will merely be *about* them. In order to enter into the theological or the philosophical, one must risk everything. The *organon* is the draught of forgetfulness.

XX

The egregore distorts the disclosure, actively seeks its disrupture. The shimmering is ignored. Denied, the invisible is not seen. Consensus asserts its will on the consent of the will-less governed. Nikolai Berdyaev: "The highly cultured man of a certain style usually expresses imitative opinions upon every subject: they are average opinions, *they belong to a group*, though it may well be that this imitativeness belongs to a cultured élite and to a highly select group."[10] The egregore speaks through the group, punishing insolence, rewarding obedience. Does the egregore create the group, or the group create the egregore?

XXI

The egregore wants to convince us that the presence we encounter in the contemplation of the phenomenon is a delusion, a form of wish-fulfilment. To assert otherwise is to invite hostility. Yet the phenomenology of this phenomenology speaks otherwise. Owen Barfield calls this "original participation." "The essence of *original participation*," he writes, "is that there stands behind the phenomena, *and on the other side of them from me*, a represented which is of the same nature as me. Whether it is called 'mana,' or by the names of many gods and demons, or God the Father, or the spirit world, it is of the same nature as the perceiving self, inasmuch as it is not mechanical or accidental, but psychic and voluntary."[11]

---

10. Nicolai Berdyaev, *Slavery and Freedom,* trans. R.M. French (New York: Scribner's, 1944), 123. My emphasis.

11. Owen Barfield, *Saving the Appearances: A Study in Idolatry,* 2nd ed. (Middletown, CT: Wesleyan University Press, 1988), 42. Barfield's emphasis.

XXII

The scientific revolution has, among others, two important legacies: the one pragmatic, the other metaphysical. Its pragmatics explore substances and processes, discern rules (*regula*) and propensities, articulate properties and quanta. Its metaphysics, however, is denied. That is: science disowns its own metaphysics, leaving it exposed as ancient Greeks would a deformed child. Realms of meaning, quality, significance: abandoned. True, a new world is created, but the scientific scheme (and it is only a scheme) is "a world of shadows."[12] Oedipus, left exposed by Laius, returned to kill his father. He was driven "by fate," the myth tells us, but, we could add, also "by instinct," as fate and instinct intersect in psychic upheavals of retribution. Oedipus's later blindness pays merciless witness to a weighty doctrine of signatures. Something eventually arrives to expose the scheme that sought resolution in exposure. The abandonment of metaphysics eventually results in tragedies of existential parricide and incest, violations of the proper order of things, and their punishment. Abandonment is one thing; nonexistence quite another.

XXIII

Phenomenology, as Husserl asserted, truly is *first philosophy*. In the context of literary studies, it is also *first criticism*. And it needs to be admitted, then, that phenomenology is also *first theology*. For what is phenomenology but pure perception of and unmediated entrance into the absolute subject of theology?

XXIV

Phänomenologie: the logos of showing forth.
At least part of the disparagement aimed at phenomenology from other philosophical/political schools arises, I think, from the discomfort implicit in "a logos of showing forth" which confronts those ill-prepared or ill-disposed to admit the possibility of a showing forth. For them, this sounds too much like religion or, even

12. A.S. Eddington, *The Nature of the Physical World* (Cambridge: Cambridge University Press, 1928), 106.

more suspect, mysticism. They have a point. But the point is only valid if we agree that there are limits to philosophy—or limits to any science. When the phenomenon discloses itself, making visible the invisible, are we culturally obligated to divert our gaze, as if present before a nursing mother? This makes no sense to me. The obligation, obviously, is to acknowledge the disclosure. "This world with all it discloses and all it conceals," writes Edith Stein, "it is just this world that also points to him who 'mysteriously reveals himself' through it."[13] How many readers of this sentence—in this instance of disclosure—have already diverted their gaze?

XXV

The poem, the text, enters into me as I enter into it: a chiastic movement of sublimation. I am sublimated: sublimated is the poem. By what? By whom? Each preserves its physicality—the paper, the flesh—yet each is transfigured, illumined, in the opening of an interior. Am I doing this? Is the poem? Whose is the initial movement? If I plant a seed, do I make it grow?

XXVI

The words of Rilke: "*Gesang ist Dasein.*" Song is Being. We cannot transform everything into Being. But we can transform everything into song. This is your task.

---

13. Edith Stein, *Knowledge and Faith*, trans. Walter Redmond (Washington, DC: ICS Publications, 2000), 99.

The Appearing: Sophiology, Poetry, and the Call for an Absolute Catholic Phenomenology

THAT Things can reveal themselves to us as they are, not only in their physicality but, more importantly, in their being, is an essential insight of phenomenology. This appearing likewise constitutes an integral phenomenal quality of religious experience and, as this chapter will argue, of sophiology. As Martin Heidegger (among others) has observed, poetry, the articulation of the poetic (here conceived more broadly than in the context of verse alone), is the paradigmatic site for such an appearing. My venture here is to suggest that the twentieth-century advent of phenomenology in the West was complemented by the arrival of sophiology (particularly in its iterations brought forth by Sergei Bulgakov and Pavel Florensky) in the East and that both can only be fully realized, and their catholicity achieved, by their being taken up by a poetic utterance fully articulated in a Catholic, sacramental metaphysics. It's not that I'm proposing a marriage between phenomenology and sophiology. My claim is that they are already married.

First: phenomenology. In the record of her conversations with him, Adelgundis Jaegerschmid recalls how Edmund Husserl's insights regarding phenomenology were both ontologically and teleologically religious: "my philosophy, phenomenology," he is reported to have said, "is intended to be nothing but a path, a method, in order to show precisely those who have moved away from Christianity and from the Christian churches the path back to God."[1] And, as he confessed to Edith Stein, "I have attempted to get through to the end without the help of theology, its proofs and its

1. Adelgundis Jaegerschmid, "Conversations with Edmund Husserl, 1931–1938," trans. Marcus Brainard, *New Yearbook for Phenomenology and Phenomenological Philosophy* 1 (2001): 331–50, at 342.

methods; in other words, I have wanted *to attain God without God*.[2] (Dominique Janicaud attempts to trouble this notion by pointing to Husserl's remark from 1935 that if phenomenology leads to God, "its road to God would be a road toward an atheistic God"[3]—but Husserl's conversion to Christianity in 1935 certainly troubles Janicaud's project.) Such a desire is certainly not explicit in Husserl's public writings, wherein God or religion are rarely mentioned, but such a phenomenon, an experience, is certainly implicit in the phenomenological act itself, despite Janicaud's assertions. Nevertheless, it was as a science (*Wissenschaft*) that Husserl presented phenomenology (a mistake echoed by his more esoteric contemporary and fellow student of Brentano's, Rudolf Steiner, who called his method *Geisteswissenschaft*).

This avoidance of "the God question" among early phenomenologists was given the lie by the—somewhat staggering given their predispositions, but understandable to anyone who has ever persevered in the praxis of phenomenological reduction over time—numerous accounts of phenomenologists turning to religion, in particular to forms of orthodox (or, more rarely, heterodox) Christianity. Indeed, Max Scheler, Edith Stein, Adolf Reinach, Hedwig Conrad-Martius, Dietrich von Hildebrand, to which one could add both Karol Wojtyla and Rudolf Steiner, all came to profoundly religious—and profoundly Christian—insights as a result of their phenomenological investigations. To sum up: there has been no "religious turn" in phenomenology. Rather, phenomenology *is* an inherently religious turn in and of itself.

This development, I think, has everything to do with the way the phenomenological reduction allows Things to speak for themselves without the baggage of colonization so characteristic of other modes of inquiry (whether it be the organons of feminist or Marxist theory, for instance; whether its stance is more in allegiance with Bacon or

---

2. Quoted in Emmanuel Falque, *God, the Flesh, and the Other: From Irenaeus to Duns Scotus*, trans. William Christian Hackett (Evanston, IL: Northwestern University Press, 2015), 78.

3. Dominique Janicaud, *Phenomenology "Wide Open": After the French Debate*, trans. Charles N. Cabral (New York: Fordham University Press, 2005), 23.

Kant). That is to say that the contemplative stance is far purer, far more integrative than any other approach, and this despite what I would call phenomenology's employment of the technology of intentionality, or, as Heidegger has written, "the setting in order of everything that presences as standing-reserve."[4] For, at the very least, the phenomenological reduction (*epoché*) is a technology, an appropriation, an apprehension, a taking-hold-of (albeit less violent than other methods). However, the technology of intentionality, as it is employed in the phenomenological reduction, only bears fruit when it is relinquished or forgotten.

It is my claim that when intentionality is relinquished or forgotten that the phenomenological reduction then metamorphoses into contemplation (*theoria*); a contemplation, according to Plotinus, from which all things arise and in which all things truly have being (*Enneads* 3.8.7). This notion bears some resemblance to Marvin Shaw's concept of the "paradox of intention," but I don't think they are identical concepts.[5] Nevertheless, it is my intention to follow this trace along another pathway, and argue that it is precisely by way of this metamorphosis into contemplation that phenomenology enters into the sophiological.

As has often been noted, a series of religious experiences drew Sergei Bulgakov, for a time an atheist and a Marxist, back to the religion of his fathers and, eventually, to the Orthodox priesthood. These religious experiences brought Bulgakov to an explicitly sophianic understanding of the world. The first such experience was inspired by the splendor of the natural world as he travelled across the steppes and took in a majestic view of the Caucasus at sunset. "Suddenly, in that evening hour," he writes,

> my soul was joyfully stirred. I started to wonder what would happen if the cosmos were not a desert and its beauty not a mask of deception—if nature were not death, but life. If he existed, the

4. Martin Heidegger, "The Turning," in *The Question Concerning Technology and other Essays* by Martin Heidegger, trans. William Lovitt (New York: Harper Torchbooks, 1977), 37.

5. Marvin C. Shaw, *The Paradox of Intention: Reaching the Goal by Giving Up the Attempt to Reach It* (Atlanta, GA: Scholars Press, 1988).

merciful and loving Father, if nature was the vesture of his love and glory, and if the pious feelings of my childhood, when I used to live in his presence, when I loved him and trembled because I was weak, were true, then the tears and inspiration of my adolescence, the sweetness of my prayers, my innocence, and all those emotions which I had rejected and trodden down would be vindicated, and my present outlook with its emptiness and deadness would appear nothing more than blindness and lies, and what a transformation it would bring to me![6]

As an aside, it is worth noting that the natural world often plays a role in the religious experiences of visionary children: the Virgin appearing above a tree to the children at Fatima; St. Michael likewise appearing to St. Joan of Arc before a venerable oak; or even the Virgin's appearance to St. Bernadette Soubirous in a garbage dump that eventually led to the discovery of a hidden spring famous throughout the world for its miraculous healings. Indeed, especially in the case of Bernadette and the spring at Lourdes, are these not sophiology's promises made manifest, the Wisdom of God shining through nature?

Three years following his Caucasian experience, Bulgakov's conversion further unfolded in Dresden, as he contemplated Raphael's *Sistine Madonna*:

> The eyes of the Heavenly Mother who holds in her arms the Eternal Infant, pierced my soul. I cried joyful and yet bitter tears, and with them the ice melted from my soul, and some of my psychological knots were loosened. This was an aesthetic emotion, but it was also a new knowledge; it was a miracle. I was then still a Marxist, but I was obliged to call my contemplation of the Madonna by the name of "prayer." I went to the Zwinger Gallery early in the mornings to pray and weep in front of the Virgin.[7]

---

6. Sergius Bulgakov, *A Bulgakov Anthology: Sergius Bulgakov 1871–1944*, trans. Natalie Duddington and James Pain, ed. James Pain and Nicolas Zernov (London: SPCK, 1976), 10–11.

7. Sergius Bulgakov, *A Bulgakov Anthology*, 11. There seems to have been a long-running Russian fascination with Raphael's famous painting by the time Bulgakov arrived. See Irene Pearson, "Raphael as Seen by Russian Writers from Zhukovsky to Turgenev," *Slavonic and East European Review* 39, no. 3 (July 1981): 346–69.

After another religious experience connected with a visit to Hagia Sophia, Bulgakov finally returned to full communion with the Church and was ordained a priest in 1918.

Now, it goes without saying that Bulgakov in these experiences was not engaging in the methodological process known as the phenomenological reduction (*epoché*), in the spirit of Husserl's *Wissenschaft*. Nevertheless, each of the phenomena in question undoubtedly disclosed themselves to Bulgakov (or were disclosed to him, if one prefers the scientific impartiality of the passive voice). They also, it could be argued, disclosed more than themselves.

So. This appearing. What is it?

First of all, I think it must be admitted that this appearing affirms a kind of sacramental epistemology: the supernatural (or something very redolent of it) shines through the natural as certain phenomena unfold themselves before us, what Gabriel Marcel called "the exigence of God . . . the exigence of transcendence disclosing its true face, a face that was shown to us before shrouded in veils."[8] It does not occur with everything, however, as in the case of the artificial, for instance, or the pornographic. Yet, upon occasion, it shines. *Splendor.* Is there any other way to put it? This phenomenological discovery of the sacramental nature of the world in all its experiential wonder, the sacramental nature of phenomena revealed supernaturally: this is how phenomenology enters the sophiological and affirms a very Catholic understanding of the world. Of course, this doesn't preclude a non-Catholic phenomenology, but to deny what I am calling the sacramental nature of this event is to deny phenomenology itself. Otherwise, no one would care. No one would enter the praxis of the *epoché*. No one would acknowledge the shining that occurs. Some do avoid this, of course. Indeed, many do. But not everyone. Furthermore, what unfolds before us in some instances is not only the phenomena themselves, but something beyond them, a phenomenon behind the phenomena, palpable evidence of a Catholic, sacramental metaphysics; indeed, of a Catholicism inherent to

8. Gabriel Marcel, *The Mystery of Being 2: Faith and Reality*, trans. René Hague (Chicago: Henry Regnery Company, 1960), 4.

the structure of the cosmos, even down to the chemical and biological levels.

The Catholicism I here invoke is not that of a doctrinaire confessionalism; nor does it exclude those not playing for Team Rome. Rather, this Catholicism simply acknowledges the truth. Phenomena disclose their truths to us, and, at times, a greater Truth simultaneously shines through them. This greater Truth is an echo of Him Who is the Truth. Thus Edith Stein's pronouncement upon having read the *Life* of Teresa of Avila at one sitting: "This is truth." Thus Michel Henry's attentiveness in his philosophy to a synonymous term, *Life*: the absolute locus of revelation in which all revelation is revealed.[9] Thus Rilke's intuitive utterance:

> I find you in all these myriad things
> I love and care for like a brother.
> As seed, you sun yourself in the smallest
> and in the greatest, spread generously abroad.
>
> That is the wondrous play of powers
> that move selflessly, upward and down:
> rising in the roots, dwindling in the bough
> and blooming like resurrection in the crown.[10]

Truth comes from God, is God. There is no "religious truth," "scientific truth." There is truth, though the description of that truth sometimes requires a rational language, sometimes a poetic language, and sometimes the simple and profoundly humble yet wordless language of presence. And our way of discerning it unfolds as Wisdom, whom the Lord "poured . . . out upon all his works, and upon all flesh according to his gift" (Sirach 1:10), opens it to us: in the same manner in which the Virgin opened Christ to us: in humility and joy. And, as Proverbs assures us, those who find Wisdom "shall find life, and shall have salvation from the Lord" (8:35).

---

9. Michel Henry, *I Am the Truth: Toward a Philosophy of Christianity*, trans. Susan Emanuel, Cultural Memory in the Present (Stanford: Stanford University Press, 2003), 27–32.

10. Translated by Daniel Polikoff, in *The Heavenly Country: An Anthology of Primary Sources, Poetry, and Critical Essays on Sophiology*, ed. Michael Martin (Kettering, OH: Angelico Press/Sophia Perennis, 2016), 236.

I've been contemplating, probably for years, the cries of "Wisdom! Be attentive!" which appear at several significant moments of the Byzantine liturgy. They occur, for those who may not know, at the Little Entrance, as the book of the gospels is held before the holy doors; prior to the readings of the epistle and the gospel; at the Great Entrance, as the Holy Gifts are brought to the altar; and before the recitation of the Creed. It seems to me that there is more than a little in the way of a sophianic theopoetics here, as Sophia/Wisdom (from one side) facilitates or catalyzes the graces of Christ that follow and the paying of attention (from the other side)—so crucial an element of phenomenological intentionality—brings us ourselves into the presence of the *mysterion*. (The movement is inherently reciprocal.) It will be noted that no such announcement precedes the Consecration—an important point—but following the Consecration (and the Epiclesis) the text invokes the Virgin herself in the hymn known as the *Megalynarion*, "The Magnification of Mary":

> It is truly proper to glorify you, O Theotokos,
> the ever-blessed, immaculate, and the Mother of our God.
> More honorable than the Cherubim
> and beyond compare more glorious than the Seraphim;
> who, a virgin, gave birth to God the Word,
> you, truly the Theotokos, we magnify.

Mary's participation in the Incarnation is acknowledged here, however tacitly, as participation in salvation and in the coming-into-being of the Eucharistic gift. As the Wisdom/Sophia of Proverbs and Sirach participates in the Creation, the Virgin participates in the Redemption of that same Creation.[11]

My investigation here is not about the liturgy, however, but about the ways in which phenomenology and sophiology discover the same phenomenon: the shining that illuminates the cosmos. This shining speaks in the languages of poetry, languages that take on a myriad of forms and are sometimes mistaken for science, sometimes for theology. As Martin Heidegger has it, "All reflective think-

---

11. This is one of the essential insights of Jacob Boehme's sophiology.

ing is poetic, and all poetry in turn is a kind of thinking."[12] This thinking distinguishes itself, I would further argue, by attentiveness to what von Balthasar identified as the Glory of the Lord, a deeply sophiological term. Furthermore, such an approach is profoundly antithetical to some ways of doing theology. As von Balthasar writes,

> In Neoscholasticism, when the feeling for the glory of God was lost—that glory which pervades Revelation as a whole but which is not perceived by conceptual rationalism, or concerning which it remains silent, or which it wholly removes by means of method—there perished also the sensorium for the glory of Creation (as "aesthetics") which shone through the whole theology of the Fathers and of the Early and High Middle Ages. This sensorium passed preeminently to the poets and artists (from Dante to Petrarch, to Milton, Herder, Hölderlin, Keats...), but also to the great natural scientists (such as Kepler and Newton, the early Kant, Goethe, Carus, Fechner, Teilhard), whereby Neoscholasticism found itself doubly bereft and denuded.[13]

This Glory is accessible to children—the formal employment of the technology provided by the *epoché* is by no means requisite—as Robert Kelly describes in the opening lines of his magnificent prose poem, "The Heavenly Country":

> Once I thought it was the place my father brought me and my mother to, between the rivers up north. The near river was full of white stones bleached in the sun, and the banks on the far side were red clay. At night it was almost cold, so we slept with blankets or walked out in sweaters early morning to see deer or whatever else might reveal itself to us. That it is a matter of It willing to reveal to Us I have never doubted.[14]

This is an eminently Catholic, eminently sacramental, and essentially sophiological insight. And we all innately possess it; it is part of

12. Martin Heidegger, *On the Way to Language*, trans. Peter D. Hertz (New York: Harper Collins, 1971), 136.

13. Hans Urs von Balthasar, *The Glory of the Lord: A Theological Aesthetics*, vol. 5: *The Realm of Metaphysics in the Modern Age*, trans. Oliver Davies et al. (San Francisco: Ignatius Press, 1991), 26–27.

14. From *The Convections* by Robert Kelly (Santa Barbara, CA: Black Sparrow Books, 1977). Also included in Michael Martin (ed.), *The Heavenly Country*.

our baptismal birthright. Only, I think, we are trained out of it through the deadening course of our education, perhaps the most invisible yet destructive of modernity's many tragedies. My late colleague, Stratford Caldecott, devoted much of his career to exploring a remedy for this poison. For him, as for me, this remedy can only be realized through an education attentive to the Glory of the World; that is, an education that simultaneously speaks the languages of rationality, theology, and poetry: in every sense of the word a truly Catholic language. This is a Catholicism hinted at in the Wisdom literature, literally fleshed out in the New Testament, and—following the collapse of traditional metaphysics in a postmodern, post-capitalistic, post-Christian, and (increasingly) post-human cultural milieu—a Catholicism that offers a much-needed corrective to the bastardization of ontology, the technological and ideological colonization of the human person, and the ascendance of postmodern nominalism so prevalent at our own cultural moment.

George Herbert and
the Phenomenology of Grace

"Thus grace constitutes the most proper depth of the will—*interior intimo meo*—as well as its most intimate stranger."

Jean-Luc Marion[1]

IN BOTH its architecture and in what can be called its metaphysical substance, George Herbert's *The Temple* is a profound and extended contemplation of the ways in which God works in (and into) the life of the Christian. In a manner perhaps unique in devotional poetry, in this carefully structured collection of poems Herbert attempts to transcend theological debate and, instead, strives to disclose the immanental qualities and experiences of a life in God, particularly in his poetic illustrations of the movements and permutations of grace. Herbert's spirituality is thoroughly *enstatic*, a term used by the Victorine theologian Thomas Gallus (c. 1200–1246) to describe a spiritual state in which "Still contained within itself and sober, the soul yet desires that which exceeds its capacities and, indeed, even its nature."[2] As opposed to ecstatic varieties of spirituality which take the believer out of him- or herself, Herbert's modest method of approaching God requires that he abide in himself, attending to and awaiting on the movements of grace when and as they come. *The Temple*, then, functions as a kind of spiritual picture book providing illustrations—and not explanations—of God's gentle theo-phantic entrances into the life of the Christian, tracing a simultaneously languaged and existential event that could be called "a chiastic point

1. Jean-Luc Marion, *Prolegomena to Charity*, trans. Stephen Lewis (New York: Fordham University Press, 2002), 65.
2. Boyd Taylor Coolman, "The Medieval Affective Dionysian Tradition" in *Rethinking Dionysius the Areopagite*, ed. Sarah Coakley and Charles M. Stang (Oxford: Wiley-Blackwell, 2009), 85–102, at 93.

where two extremes cross paths."[3] Taking a phenomenological reading of Herbert as my starting point, in this chapter I explore Herbert's *The Temple* as a space for a variety of encounters with God, encounters figured by a *double intentionality*: from Herbert's (the speaker's) side showing the struggles, anxieties, and uncertainties attendant to religious belief; and from "God's side" disclosing a "phenomenology of grace." By calling what I find in Herbert a "phenomenology of grace," however, I do not mean to suggest that the poet was working in a Husserlian idiom *avant le lettre*, but, rather, that he was exploring the ways in which grace actually unfolds in the lives of believers, in grace as phenomenon. In his attention to the phenomenology of grace, Herbert opens for his reader an opportunity for thinking about the possibility of religious experience and, in at least one documented case, access to religious experience itself. Like prayer, Herbert's poetry is nothing if not a dialogue with the absolutely Other.

Surprised by Grace

One of the ways that Herbert figures grace in the poems of *The Temple* is in the "element of surprise" that inhabits the verse. As readers of Herbert are familiar, nearly every poem in the collection somewhere holds a surprise, an "aha!" moment, so much so that the reader anticipates it. This phenomenon is most apparent in the visual poems, such as "The Altar" and "Easter Wings," whose clever construction and obvious charm awaken delight in the reader, a strategy also present in less anthologized poems such as "The Watercourse," "Ana-{Mary/Army}gram," and "Jesu." "Colossians 3:3" performs a similar trick, showing how grace lies within the larger forum of what is ostensibly a rather straightforward stanza block. Indeed, the very "blockiness" of "Colossians 3:3" and the grace-full message contained within it work together to unfold this religious

3. John P. Manoussakis, "The Phenomenon of God: From Husserl to Marion," *American Catholic Philosophical Quarterly* 78, no. 1 (2004): 53–68, at 62. Manoussakis employs the term "inverse intentionality" to describe a phenomenon very similar to what I call "double intentionality" in the present essay.

sensibility: that grace can be found, not only in the extraordinary (as in the more charmingly shaped poems) but also in the seeming ordinary. This is also the case in "Paradise," with its incremental pruning of letters from the final word of each stanza's first line in order reveal an insight hidden within the word. This religious aesthetic is most explicitly illustrated in the poem's fourth stanza, which moves from a contemplation of reduction and sacrifice ("SPARE", "PARE") to a discovery of being ("ARE"):

> When thou dost greater judgements SPARE,
> And with thy knife but prune and PARE,
> Ev'n fruitfull trees more fruitfull ARE. (10–12)

These poems unfold an immanent quality in writing, in nature, in language itself, and, even, in alleged human agency: God and God's grace lurk within creation—in terms of human art as well as of the natural world—and spring forth in moments of surprise and insight, of reassurance and delight. Despite Herbert's habitual meditations on affliction and suffering, these moments of grace in the poems disclose God's portion not only in the writing of them, but, more importantly for George Herbert the pastor, they also illustrate God's activity in the life of the Christian.

Another clever—and very subtle—manipulation of structure comes in the sonnet "H. Baptisme (I)." Here, Herbert modifies the conventional structure of the sonnet form to lead the reader into a cosmological-theological meditation on both the baptism of Christ and the baptism of the Christian.

H. Baptisme (I)

> As he that sees a dark and shadie grove,
> Stayes not, but looks beyond it on the skie;
> So when I view my sinnes, mine eyes remove
> More backward still, and to the water flie,
> Which is above the heav'ns, whose spring and vent
> Is in my deare Redeemers pierced side.
> O blessed streams! either ye do prevent
> And stop our sinnes from growing thick and wide,
> Or else give tears to drown them, as they grow.

In you Redemption measures all my time,
And spreads the plaister equall to the crime.
You taught the Book of Life my name, that so
What ever future sinnes should me miscall,
Your first acquaintance might discredit all.

The interesting thing about this sonnet is that it is backward. The volta, which traditionally comes after the eighth line, here appears following the sixth, which Herbert accentuates with the exclamation "O blessed streams!"[4] So, irrespective of the rhyme scheme, the sestet comes first, followed by the octave. This shift in perspective coincides with the poem's argument. The opening lines feature an observer of heaven. Quickly the speaker's attention turns to the water "above the heav'ns" descending from Christ. Then, rather than the observer seeking heaven, heaven comes to the observer, performing a kind of poetic "contrary motion," an idea Herbert would have known from his proficiency in music. When he writes "more backward still" (line 4), Herbert not only constructs a line of verse, but he also wryly comments on his aesthetic for the poem.

The notion also has theological significance, and one which Herbert would have encountered in Aquinas's *Catena aurea*, the collection of biblical commentary the Angelic Doctor collected from the Church Fathers—a handy resource for a preacher like Herbert. *Catena aurea*, along with Lyra's *Postilla litteralis super totam bibliam* (1322–31) and the *Glossa ordinaria* (12th c.), was one of the most popular patristic resources consulted by early modern preachers.[5]

---

4. Sir Philip Sidney, among others, also played with reverse sonnets in, for instance, *Astrophil and Stella* 39, "Come Sleep, the certain know of peace." See *Sir Philip Sidney's An Apology for Poetry and Astrophil and Stella: Texts and Contexts*, ed. Peter C. Herman (Glen Allen, VA: College Publishing, 2001).

5. Katrin Ettenhuber, "The Preacher and Patristics" in *The Oxford Handbook of the early Modern Sermon*, ed. Peter McCullough, Hugh Adlington, and Emma Rhatigan (Oxford: Oxford University Press), 34–53, at 39. *Catena aurea* was popular from the Middle Ages through the early modern period. An edition appeared in the early seventeenth century as *Catena aurea, in Matthaeum, Marcum, Lucam et Joannem ex Sanctorum patrum sententiis* (Antverpiae: Apud Ioannem Keerbergium, anno 1612).

Herbert's friend John Donne sometimes turned to Aquinas's colla-
tion, so it is not much of a stretch to suggest that Herbert did as
well.[6] In the book, Aquinas includes a passage attributed to Augustine's teacher Ambrose on Matthew's account of Christ's baptism
(Matt 3:13–15):

> Scripture tells of many wonders wrought at various times in this
> river; as that, among others, in the Psalms, *Jordan, was driven
> backwards*; [Ps. 114:3] before the water was driven back, now sins
> are turned back in its current; as Elijah divided the waters of old,
> so Christ the Lord wrought in the same Jordan the separation of
> sin.[7]

In both Herbert's poem and in Ambrose's commentary, *sins* are
held in check or driven backward in baptism. In addition, the
"blessed streams" of Herbert's poem also have Eucharistic implications, being derived, as they are, from the "Redeemers pierced side"
(line 6). Herbert turns the theological and mystical insight of
Ambrose into a clever performative strategy for constructing the
poetry of religious experience.

The Still, Small Voice

A second way in which Herbert figures the movement of grace in
the poems of *The Temple* comes in his representations of the experience of theophantic insight, the manifestation of the "still, small
voice." Herbert's template for the experience is derived from 1
Kings, Elijah's experience of the presence of God through a whisper,
and not through the pyrotechnics of earthquake and fire: "And,
behold, the Lord passed by, and a great and strong wind rent the
mountains, and brake in pieces the rocks before the Lord; but the
Lord was not in the wind: and after the wind an earthquake; but the
Lord was not in the earthquake: And after the earthquake a fire; but

6. Katrin Ettenhuber, *Donne's Augustine: Renaissance Cultures of Interpretation*
(Oxford: Oxford University Press, 2011), 88–89.

7. S. Thomas Aquinas, *Catena Aurea: Commentary of the Four Gospels Collected
out of the Works of the Fathers*, 4 vols., 2nd ed. (Oxford: John Henry and James
Parker, 1864), vol. 1, part 1:108.

the Lord was not in the fire: and after the fire a still small voice" (1 Kings 19:11–12).[8] Some poems in *The Temple* feature God as the sole speaker, as is the case with "The Sacrifice," "An Offering," and, at second hand, "The Pulley." Others feature a dialectical tension between God and the human speaker, as with "Dialogue," "The Banquet," and perhaps most powerfully in "Love (III)." But with the "still, small voice" convention, Herbert figures the entrance of God into the poem and into both the speaker's and, importantly, the reader's awareness. In these poems, God, as it were, takes over the poem from the speaker, illustrating Herbert's understanding of at least one way God interacts with the believer. But Herbert cannot make these theophanies, these presences (*parousia*) of God, work rhetorically without also providing a poetic framework depicting God's absences.

In his contemplation of the presence/absence tension present in the Christian's relationship to God, Herbert, as Rosemond Tuve has argued, draws upon medieval mystical and poetic traditions grounded in the religious aesthetic found in the Song of Songs.[9] In the Song, for instance, the female Lover finds herself in a great deal of anguish due to the Beloved's disappearance: "I opened to my beloved; but my beloved had withdrawn himself, and was gone: my soul failed when he spake: I sought him, but I could not find him; I

---

8. Authorized Version.

9. The first collection of poetry published in English, indeed, was William Baldwin's *Canticles, or Balades of Salomon* (1549), and Noam Flinker suggests the volume had a direct influence on Herbert's religious poetics. See Flinker's *The Song of Songs in English Renaissance Literature: Kisses of Their Mouths* (Cambridge: D.S. Brewer, 2000), 31–32. In England, no less than one hundred-thirty editions of commentaries, sermons, paraphrases, or poetic renderings of the Song of Songs found their way into publication between 1549 and 1700, many of them in octavo format, making them accessible to the faithful of modest means. And the work's popularity was not limited to the early modern period. Jean Leclerq calls the text "the most read and most frequently commented on in the medieval cloister." See his *The Love of Learning and the Desire for God: A Study in Monastic Culture*, trans. Catherine Misrahi (1961; reprt., New York: Fordham University Press, 1982), 106. Christian commentaries on the Song began in the late classical period with Origen (c. 185–254) and perhaps reached their height with Bernard of Clairvaux's (1090–1153) monumental version.

called him, but he gave me no answer" (5:6). Herbert voices a similar sentiment in "Deniall":

> As good go any where, they say,
> As to benumme
> Both knees and heart, in crying night and day,
> *Come, come, my God, O come,*
> But no hearing. (11–15)

The speaker's anxiety is palpable, and Herbert emphasizes this anxiety by the repetition of "But no hearing," the only reoccurring line in the poem. The agony of separation from God only adds power to the speaker's metaphysical desire when communion with the divine finally arrives, as Herbert writes in "The Glimpse," "Thy short abode and stay / Feeds not, but adds to the desire of meat" (11–12) with its obvious Eucharistic overtones.

One of the clearest poetic expositions of the absence/presence dynamic in *The Temple* appears in "The Search." In this poem, Herbert borrows heavily from the Song of Songs, echoing its sweet despair of anxious separation:

> Whither, O, wither art thou fled,
> My Lord, my Love?
> My searches are my daily bread;
> Yet never prove. (1–4)

This absence, however, bears with it a grief which nevertheless connects the speaker to God,

> Since then my grief must be as large,
> As is thy space,
> Thy distance from me; see my charge,
> Lord, see my case. (45–48)

In the poem (and in a good deal of Christian mysticism) God's presence underlies his absences—the one implies the other, and, eventually, as the poet and preacher phrases it, a tangible assurance arrives, "Making two one" (line 60). This is the assurance at which the Herbertian speaker arrives in this poem, but "Longing," a poem that occurs earlier in the sequence of *The Temple*, painfully lacks assurance.

"Longing" is, appropriately, one of the longer poems in the collection, eighty-four lines of the speaker's Job-like lamentation over God's absence and seeming indifference. It opens in despair and complaint:

> With sick and famisht eyes,
> With doubling knees and weary bones,
> To thee my cries,
> To thee my grones,
> To thee my sighs, my tears ascend:
> No end? (1–6)

From despair and complaint the poem moves on—to more despair and complaint. The poem, indeed, is, in its length and painful irresolution, performative of its title. The speaker's despair borders on blasphemy as he accuses his God:

> Thou tariest, while I die,
> And fall to nothing: thou dost reigne,
> And rule on high,
> While I remain
> In bitter grief: yet am I stil'd
> Thy childe. (54–60)

Unlike most of the poems in *The Temple*, "Longing" has no moment of respite, no turn of grace that offers consolation to the speaker (or reader). Instead, the poem ends with an entreaty that God "heal my troubled breast which cryes, / Which dyes" (83–84).

Herbert Grierson has observed that "the central theme" of Herbert's poetry "is the psychology of his religious experiences."[10] This is a valuable insight, but I think "phenomenology of his religious experiences" is more to the point. Interpreting them as purely psychological implies a kind of spiritual self-centeredness, which is not at all what interests Herbert. Herbert crafted and arranged *The Temple*, at the very least, with pastoral care in mind: he is concerned with showing his readers—perhaps even more than he is with showing himself—the way God works in human life,[11] another rea-

---

10. Herbert J.C. Grierson, Introduction. *Metaphysical Lyrics and Poems of the Seventeenth Century: Donne to Butler* (Oxford: The Clarendon Press, 1921), xlii.

son to resist a "psychological" reading. This is why Herbert's themes echo and reverberate throughout the sequence, disclosing a method in which they "acquire meaning from their relations and interactions with each other."[12] Indeed, "The Bag," the poem immediately following "Longing," opens with the words "Away despair! my gracious Lord doth heare" (1), speaking directly to the dramatic situation of "Longing." Clearly, Herbert arranged this section of *The Temple* (and others) with all the deliberation and foresight of a playwright, and what he says of the Bible in "The H. Scriptures (II)" can easily be said for *The Temple* as a whole: "This verse marks that, and both do make a motion / Unto a third, that ten leaves off doth lie" (5–6). After "The Bag" follows "The Jews," a short poem that allows the poetic tension to settle before it returns *en force* in "The Collar."[13] It is no accident that the despair of "Longing" resurfaces three poems later in "The Collar." But in "The Collar," unlike "Longing," the despair morphs into open hostility toward the silent divinity—and then comes to a most startling resolution.

"The Collar" is one of Herbert's most anthologized poems and one which has received an extraordinary amount of critical attention over the years. As Louis Martz has noticed, "The Collar" opens in a mood of open blasphemy and unfolds in a perversion of Eucharistic imagery.[14] F. E. Hutchinson called the poem, somewhat anachronistically, an "early example of *vers libre*,"[15] a reading Joseph Summers famously rejected, describing the poem instead as an experi-

11. Ramie Targoff rightly observes that "in poem and after poem of *The Temple*, the speaker intertwines the expression of his inner self with the creation of skillful texts that might be shared by fellow worshippers." See her *Common Prayer: The Language of Public Devotion in Early Modern England* (Chicago: The University of Chicago Press, 2001), 88.

12. James Boyd White, *"This Book of Starres": Learning to Read George Herbert* (Ann Arbor: University of Michigan Press, 1994), 153.

13. Martz examines the structural relationships of this sequence in *The Poetry of Meditation: A Study in English Religious Literature of the Seventeenth Century*, 2nd ed. (New Haven: Yale University Press, 1962), 300–04.

14. Ibid., 303.

15. F. E. Hutchinson, Introduction, *The Works of George Herbert*, ed. by F. E. Hutchinson (Oxford: The Clarendon Press, 1941), 530. All quotes from Herbert are from this edition.

ment in "hieroglyphic form."[16] Herbert's speaker rages throughout the poem. He accuses God of abandonment and indifference, "Is the yeare onely lost to me? / Have I no bayes to crown it?" (14–15). Furthermore, the speaker abandons notions of both virtue and sinfulness: "leave thy cold dispute," he tells himself, "Of what is fit, and not. Forsake thy cage" (20–21), the cage in question here the Church as well as the priesthood. Herbert figures here a state of hot rebellion, as his insolent speaker dares God to prove himself. But, then, the still small voice arrives:

> But as I rav'd and grew more fierce and wilde
> At every word,
> Me thoughts I heard one calling, *Child!*
> And I reply'd, *My Lord.* (33–35)

God's intrusion into the poem and into the life of the speaker is not a consequence of the speaker's rational assessment of the situation, nor is it a result of the speaker's pragmatic acceptance of things as they are, nor an answer to prayer, and it is certainly not due to merit. Indeed, there is no *reason* why the poem, according to its own emotional trajectory, should end in this way and so abruptly. Throughout the poem the speaker grows "more fierce and wilde / At every word," including *the* Word. The speaker, then, according to his behavior, clearly does not deserve that God should grant him comfort. But God nevertheless does, freely bestowing grace on his suffering servant with only a single word, "Child," which is why Herbert transforms the near blasphemy of the rage against the word / Word by rhyming it with "Lord," uttered by the speaker under the influence of this sanctifying grace.[17] An effective way to

16. Joseph H. Summers, *George Herbert: His Religion and Art* (Cambridge: Harvard University Press, 1968), 90. Summers admires the way Herbert's chaotic structure of long and short lines combined with the erratic rhyme scheme figure the emotional and spiritual "anarchy" the speaker religious/existential turmoil in the poem. See 90–92; 138.

17. Richard Hooker describes the grace of sanctification (or, alternately, the grace of regeneration) as the state in which God participates in human life. "Seeing therefore that Christ is in us as a quickning Spirit, the first degree of Communion with Christ must needs consist in the Participation of his Spirit." See Richard Hooker, *The Lawes of Ecclesial Polity*, 5.56.

figure grace and inner communion with God, Herbert also utilizes the still, small voice in "Jordan (II)." But one of his more startling uses of the figure appears in "Artillerie" where Herbert plays against his own still, small voice convention, figuring a kind of spiritual experience with a very different interlocutor.

The critical history of "Artillerie" is relatively skimpy, though both Richard Strier and Michael Schoenfeldt have given the poem some attention, the former reading it as Herbert's argument against rationalism in matters of faith[18] and the latter questioning the appropriation of military terminology as a mode for treating the "negotiations that occur between mortals and God."[19] Unlike "The Collar" and "Jordan (II)," the disembodied voice of "Artillerie" does not arrive with the spiritual resolution of a conflict at the end of the poem, but is accompanied by very real (though metaphoric) fireworks in the first stanza:

> As I one ev'ning sat before my cell,
> Me thoughts a starre did shoot into my lap.
> I rose, and shook my clothes, as knowing well,
> That from small fires comes oft no small mishap.
> *When suddenly I heard one say,*
> *Do as thou usest, disobey,*
> *Expell good motions from thy breast,*
> *Which have the face of fire, but end in rest.* (1–8)

The words uttered by the voice here do not sound very "God-ly." Indeed, they come off as cavalier, a little sarcastic, absolutely counter to what one would expect from a loving God. Hutchinson reads the falling star of "Artillerie" as a "divine impulse," made of fire and, therefore, suggestive of "danger and disturbance,"[20] whereas Robert Ellrodt sees God as the co-speaker.[21] A close reading of the poem, however, points in another direction. My contention is that the voice

---

18. Richard Strier, *Love Known: Theology and Experience in George Herbert's Poetry* (Chicago: The University of Chicago Press, 1983), 99.

19. Michael C. Schoenfeldt, *Prayer and Power: George Herbert and Renaissance Courtship* (Chicago: The University of Chicago Press, 1991), 193.

20. *Works*, 526.

21. Robert Ellrodt, *Seven Metaphysical Poets: A Structural Study of the Unchanging Self* (Oxford: Oxford University Press, 2000), 49.

does not belong to God. Rather, the speaker here is Lucifer, the fallen angel, in the guise of a fallen star. The poem clearly alludes to the "falling star" Lucifer of Isaiah and Luke: "How art thou fallen from heaven, O Lucifer, son of the morning! how art thou cut down to the ground, which didst weaken the nations!" (Is 14:12) and "I beheld Satan as lightning fall from heaven" (Lk 10:18). This, and not a mystical dialogue with God, is the poem's *mise-en-scène*.

In the second stanza of "Artillerie," the speaker resists the invitation of the Tempter:

> I, who had heard of musick in the spheres,
> But not of speech in starres, began to muse:
> *But turning to my God*, whose ministers
> The starres and all things are; If I refuse,
>> Dread Lord, said I, so oft my good;
>> Then I refuse not ev'n with bloud
>> To wash away my stubborn thought:
> For I will do or suffer what I ought.
>> (9–16, my emphasis)

Lucifer, like Satan in the Book of Job, also works—indirectly, so to speak—under Divine Providence as "a minister" (*angelos*). If not a member in good standing, Satan, despite his cosmic demotion, is still associated with the angelic hierarchy: "Now there was a day when the sons of God came to present themselves before the Lord, and Satan came also among them" (Job 1:6). Herbert's speaker knows what he is dealing with and resists the temptation to "expel good motions" from his breast: he turns *away* from the talking star and *toward* God. This explains why Herbert's speaker is in such a hurry to shake the fallen star from his clothes, "knowing well, / That from small fires comes oft no small mishap" (lines 2–3). This is not to say that temptation is a bad thing in and of itself. As Herbert's contemporary and fellow Anglican clergyman Jeremy Taylor has it and as Herbert would have agreed, "temptation is the opportunity of virtue and a crown."[22] God allows Lucifer (pride) to tempt the

---

22. Jeremy Taylor, *The Life of Christ* in *The Whole Works of the Right Rev. Jeremy Taylor, D.D.*, ed. Reginald Heber, rev. Charles Page Eden, 10 vols. (London: Longmans, Green, & Co., 1883), 2:204.

speaker. Lucifer, then, is God's volley in the artillery of the poem. The only response the speaker can make—his "artillery"—is found in his "tears and prayers" (line 19), as temptation successfully resisted, like affliction, leads one to rely more fully on God, a theme of Herbert's verse. Importantly, for Herbert, the encounter with God, though freely bestowed on the believer, *follows* a period of spiritual struggle. It does not precede it. As 1 Kings explains it and as "Artillerie" affirms, truly, "the Lord was not in the fire." God, certainly, is present even in apparent absence, but, as Herbert suggests, the believer needs first to become aware of a need for God in order to appreciate the encounter.

Herbert and the Eucharist

The clearest examples of the Christian's encounter with God in *The Temple* are found in the many poems that describe that encounter in terms of the Eucharist. It is impossible to read through the body of poems comprising *The Temple* and avoid noticing the importance of the Eucharist to Herbert's spirituality. Though the Eucharistic aesthetic of the collection is impossible to ignore (or, perhaps, because of it) critical attention has attempted to problematize what does not appear to be very problematic. Catherine Gallagher and Stephen Greenblatt have examined the importance of debates about the nature of the Eucharist in early modern Europe, seeing in them a drive for dominance and control,[23] while Richard Strier has tried harder than most to complicate Herbert's attention to the Eucharist, interpreting Herbert as a "thoroughgoing Calvinist"[24] when it comes to the Lord's Supper. In his influential study, *Love Known: Theology and Experience in George Herbert's Poetry* (1983), Strier, in

---

23. Catherine Gallagher and Stephen Greenblatt, *Practicing New Historicism* (Chicago: The University of Chicago Press, 2000), 143–46. As Cruickshank observes, "new historicists have read the Eucharist as an analogy for the falsely hermetic art of traditional literary study: an object cut loose from temporality, process and intention, by cultural consensus miraculously or magically transcending circumstance." *Verse and Poetics*, 94.

24. Richard Strier, "George Herbert and Ironic Ekphrasis," *Classical Philology* 102, No. 1 (January 2007): 96–109, at 98.

his own words, "militates strongly against a specifically Eucharistic reading" of Herbert, while acknowledging that "Herbert frequently uses Eucharistic-sounding language—metaphorically,"[25] and the critic has stuck to these interpretive guns as recently as 2007. R. V. Young has called Strier's "Calvinist hypothesis" into question, noting, among other things, that, in addition to Herbert's preoccupation with the Eucharist, his love for formal liturgy also puts him in opposition to Calvinism's distrust of ceremony.[26] Heather Asals, similarly, has argued that Herbert's verse "is eucharistic because it concentrates the 'creature' of language as the ontological bridge to the divine"[27] and Rosemond Tuve has identified "the blood of the Eucharist" as "a mystery always to the forefront of Herbert's mind."[28] Some critics, it is true, have argued for the primacy of scripture as an influence in Herbert's poetry,[29] and while it is hard to deny the importance of the Bible to his work, such a fact should come as no surprise—and acknowledging the importance of the Bible to Herbert does absolutely nothing to diminish the importance of the Eucharist to him. Though some scholars have followed Strier,[30] the general consensus is that the Sacrament is the focal point of Herbert's religion.[31] The evidence is, quite simply, over-

---

25. Strier, *Love Known*, 46–47, note 41.

26. R. V. Young, *Doctrine and Devotion in Seventeenth-Century Poetry: Studies in Donne, Herbert, Crashaw, and Vaughan*, Studies in Renaissance Literature (Cambridge: D. S. Brewer, 2000), 116–18; 122.

27. Heather A. L. Asals, *Equivocal Predication: George Herbert's Way to God* (Toronto: University of Toronto Press, 1981), 6.

28. Rosemond Tuve, *A Reading of George Herbert* (Chicago: The University of Chicago Press, 1952), 70.

29. Chana Bloch, following the path laid by Barbara K. Lewalski, has focused on the Bible as *the* source of Herbert's heavenly muse. See her *Spelling the Word: George Herbert and the Bible* (Berkeley: University of California Press, 1985). Though she acknowledges the Eucharistic overtones in *The Temple*, she embeds them in the Bible at the expense of the liturgical life of the Church. See in particular pages 100–04.

30. Esther Gillman Richey, "The Intimate Other: Lutheran Subjectivity in Spenser, Donne, and Herbert," *Modern Philology* 108, no. 3 (February 2011): 343–74.

31. Among the studies arguing on behalf of the Eucharist as central to an understanding of Herbert are Regina M. Schwartz, *Sacramental Poetics at the Dawn of Secularism: When God Left the World*, Cultural Memory in the Present (Stanford:

whelming. As Herbert's friend Lancelot Andrewes phrased it, and as Herbert's poetry testifies, "the holy Eucharist . . . is the corner-stone of the Law and the Gospel."[32] Adding to this critical argument, my claim is that, for George Herbert, the Eucharist stands as the most tangible proof of God's presence in the world, the central and most readily available locus of grace.

Before examining the Eucharistic aesthetic Herbert upholds, it is important first to notice the difference between how wine is represented in *The Church Porch* section of *The Temple* as opposed to its many appearances in *The Church* (no reference to the Eucharist appears in *The Church Militant*). In *The Church Porch*'s "The Perirrhanterium" wine is a symbol of incontinence and a loss of self-control. "Drink not the third glasse," Herbert warns readers, "which thou canst not tame, / When once it is within thee" (25–26). Twice more he emphasizes the same notion.[33] Herbert does not see any value in wine as a symbol for spiritual inebriation as is the case in Sufi poetry and in the Christian mysticism of John Ruusbroec and Francis of Assisi, among others.[34] Herbert, grounded in an enstatic spirituality, wishes to avoid that kind of ecstatic religious experience. But the actual and metaphoric nature of wine changes once the reader enters into the precincts of both *The Church* and the Church. As the reader crosses the threshold, the poem "Superliminare," he is invited to "approach, and taste / The churches mysticall repast" (4), and the first thing seen is "The Altar."

Stanford University Press, 2008), 117–38, and Ryan Netzley, *Reading, Desire, and the Eucharist in Early Modern Religious Poetry* (Toronto: University of Toronto Press, 2011), 23–65.

32. A sermon preached 24 March 1611, in Lancelot Andrewes, *Ninety-Six Sermons*, 5 vols. (Oxford: James Parker and Co., 1871–75), 2:292.

33. "Stay at the third glasse: if thou lose thy hold, / Then thou art modest, and the wine grows bold" (41–42) and "Stay at the third cup, or forgo the place. / Wine above all things doth Gods stamp deface" (47–48).

34. John Ruusbroec, *The Spiritual Espousals and Other Works*, trans. James A. Wiseman (Mahwah: Paulist Press, 1986). Bonaventure, in his *Life of Saint Francis*, describes his subject returning from Communion "like one inebriated in spirit, and rapt out of himself in ecstasy." See Bonaventure, *The Life of St. Francis* (London: J. M. Dent and Company, 1904), 96.

There has been much debate about the significance of this poem. As Arthur L. Clements has observed, "*The Church* begins at an altar and ends at a table, another name for an altar. It begins with meditations on Christ's bloody sacrifice and ends with a celebration of his bloodless sacrifice in a contemplative Eucharistic feast [i.e., in 'Love (III)'].''[35] Many critics, however, have accepted the assertion that the altar one meets at the opening of *The Church* corresponds to the altars of the classical period which were situated closer to the entrance of a temple (and not a Christian church) and not at the opposite end of the building, what is generally referred to in church design as "the East."[36] While Herbert certainly would have appreciated the classical overtones these scholars have detected in the poem, his main intention was not to invoke the age of antiquity. If anything, he recognized antiquity as anticipating in some ways the coming of the Church: "Religion, like a pilgrime, westward bent, / Knocking at all doores, ever as she went" (*The Church Militant*, lines 29–30). But he has other things in mind with leading the reader's attention to an altar. Quite simply, the architecture of a church (and the Anglican church buildings of Herbert's time were almost entirely the Catholic churches of the pre-Reformation) is designed with the altar as *the* focal point. The altar may not be the first thing one *touches* when entering the nave, but it is surely the first thing one *sees*. And, as the body and structure of the poems repeatedly reiterate, the altar and all it signifies—Christ's sacrifice, the individual's need to approach him in the Eucharist and participate in his Mystical Body—are the reason for a church building in the first place, as Herbert implies in "The Sacrifice": "For they will pierce my side, I full well know; / That as sinne came, so Sacraments might

---

35. Arthur L. Clements, *Poetry of Contemplation: John Donne, George Herbert, Henry Vaughan, and the Modern Period* (Albany: State University of New York Press, 1990), 96.

36. Mary Ellen Rickey, *Utmost Art: Complexity in the Verse of George Herbert* (Lexington: University of Kentucky Press, 1966), 10; Summers, *Religion and Art*, 141. See also Bart Westerweel's fascinating discussion of "The Altar" in his *Patterns and Patterning: A Study of Four Poems by George Herbert* (Amsterdam: Editions Rodopi, 1984), 53–139.

flow" (146–47). Taking this into consideration, it is difficult to argue with C.A. Patrides's observation that the "Eucharist is the marrow of Herbert's sensibility."[37] On the other hand, because of the centrality of the altar and the Eucharist to the poetry, it is difficult to accept Strier's resistance to a Eucharistic reading of both Herbert and *The Temple* when he asserts that "The Altar" "does not in any way refer to the Eucharist."[38] Many of the poems in *The Temple*, on the contrary, argue that it does.

Herbert's clearest poetic exposition of the centrality of the Eucharist as a real contact with Christ and channel of grace comes in the two poems entitled "The H. Communion," one from *The Temple* and the other found only in the Williams MS. The poem from *The Temple* speaks directly to the communicant/speaker's intimacy with God at receiving the Eucharist, telling his Lord, "To me dost now thyself convey" (4). This is no memorial, but an encounter with the divine. "But by way of nourishment and strength," writes Herbert,

> Thou creep'st into my breast;
> Making thy way my rest,
> And thy small quantities my length;
> Which spread their forces into every part,
> Meeting sinnes force and art. (7–12)

Ryan Netzly has rightly argued that in this poem the poet figures "not a transcendent spirituality, but rather the very sacramental, even bodily, immanence that attends the Real Presence."[39] Herbert knows that a merely memorial Eucharist, a religious meal empty of the Real Presence, would not have the power to either bring Christ to the believer or transform the communicant in any way. Thus, he acknowledges,

---

37. C.A. Patrides, Introduction, *The English Poems of George Herbert* (London: J.M. Dent, 1974), 17.

38. Strier, *Love Known*, 191. Regina Schwartz calls Strier's anti-Eucharistic insistence into question, pointing to some comments he made during an MLA debate on *Love* in 1997. She thinks these contradicted his take in *Love Known*, which she sees as an "otherwise consonant reading of Herbert." I think he was being perfectly consistent. See her *Sacramental Poetics*, 177, note 33.

39. Netzly, *Reading, Desire, and the Eucharist*, 29.

> Only thy *grace,* which with these elements comes,
> > Knoweth the ready way,
> > And hath the privie key,
> Op'ning the souls most subtile rooms. (29–32)[40]

Not only does Eucharistic grace permeate the soul, which thereby influences the body, as a result of its sanctifying grace it also opens the gates of heaven to the communicant so that "He might to heav'n from Paradise go, / As from one room t'another. /... restor'd ... to this ease / By this thy heav'nly bloud" (35–38). Just as the profane wine depicted in the "Perirrhanterium" cannot be controlled "once it is within thee" and transforms the partaker who "forfets Man, and doth devest / All worldly right, save what he hath by beast" (35–36), so the sacramental wine of *The Church* restores the communicant: "when ever at his board / I do but taste it, straight it cleanseth me" ("Conscience," 14–15).

In "The H. Communion" poem found in the Williams MS, however, the soteriological concerns found in its companion poem in *The Temple* are pushed to the background.[41] In the Williams MS poem, which, if not an earlier work, does not seem to be as fully realized a poem as its counterpart in *The Temple* (Herbert obviously did not think it to be), the poet attends to the Sacrament as *mysterion.* The poem opens by considering how the speaker might believe in the Real Presence, "how shall I know / Whether in these gifts thou bee so / As thou art everywhere" (1–3). These lines, however, are a straw man: Herbert is not really interested in the question he poses. Rather, the poem argues for a trust in the *mysterion* of the Real Presence, not an explanation. Herbert refuses to enter into the debates over the Eucharist that so marked his age, writing in the second stanza, "ffirst I am sure, whether bread stay / Or whether Bread doe fly away / Concerneth bread, not mee" (7–9). And he further develops this notion throughout the poem, wondering in the third stanza "if that thou two stations makest / In Bread & mee" (16–17) and in

---

40. My emphasis.

41. It does not seem right to call this poem a "version" of the poem of the same name found in *The Temple,* as Netzley does in his study. They are completely different creations, save in name. See Netzley, *Reading, Desire, and the Eucharist,* 33–35.

the fourth whether "thou didst all those pains endure / To' abolish Sinn, not Wheat" (20–21). The poem never strays from these ideas and never really develops beyond them, though the fifth stanza touches on the moderately theological notion of Impanation, the understanding that the body and blood of Christ are co-substantial with the species of bread and wine (which influenced Luther's concept of Consubstantiation). Instead of entering into the fray of Eucharistic debate, Herbert concludes that *how* the Eucharistic elements become the Body and Blood of Christ is not nearly as important to know as the fact *that* they do. Thus, he ends this poem relying on trust in the Real Presence—no matter how it comes about:

> This gift of all gifts is the best,
> Thy flesh the least that I request.
>   Thou took'st that pledg from mee:
> Give me not that I had before,
> Or give me that, so I have more;
>   My God, give mee all Thee. (43–48)

Herbert—at least in these two poems—avoids committing to either the Calvinist notion that the Eucharist, though Christ's Presence is Real, is "spiritual" or the more sensuous Catholic understanding that Richard Crashaw would later exploit.

Though Ellrodt believes Herbert's "mode of apprehension" (a telling phrase) regarding the Eucharist "was truly original" and that the poet "was more precise when he suggested a parallel action of divine grace on the soul and the material elements of the body,"[42] a case can be argued that Herbert was more than a little in-line with Richard Hooker's theology. For one, Hooker does not think fretting about how the elements become the Body and Blood of Christ serves any real purpose:

> *This is my Body*, and *This is my Blood*, being words of promise, sith we all agree, That by the Sacraments, Christ doth really and truly in us, perform his promise; why do we vainly trouble our selves with so fierce Contentions, whether by Consubstantiation, or else by Transubstantiation the Sacrament it self be first possessed with

---

42. Ellrodt, *Seven Metaphysical Poets*, 210–11.

Christ, or no? A thing which no way can either further or hinder us, howsoever it stand, because our Participation of Christ in this Sacrament, dependeth on the co-operation of his Omnipotent Power, which maketh it his Body and Blood to us; whether with change or without alteration of the Element, such as they imagine, we need not greatly to care or inquire.[43]

This is a theological position also held by Donne.[44] But I fail to see how Herbert is "more precise" than Hooker. Indeed, he distinctly *avoids* precision when discussing the *mysterion*. What is important to Herbert is that the Eucharist is a locus of grace. That is all the understanding he needs, and one in accord with Hooker's position, as the latter writes in *Lawes of Ecclesial Polity*, "That saving Grace which Christ originally is, or hath for the general good of his whole Church, by Sacraments he severally deriveth into every member thereof. Sacraments serve as the Instruments of God, to that end and purpose."[45]

Despite Strier's attempt to direct critical attention toward a more Calvinist, and ultimately a more secular, read on Herbert, Herbert's spirituality, as repeatedly shown in *The Temple*, is overwhelmingly Eucharistic and, importantly, overwhelmingly mystical when it comes to the Eucharist. This is not to say that Herbert is a "mystic" in the traditional sense of the word. Strier likes to think of Herbert's "distrust of reason and ingenuity" as informed by Luther and Calvin,[46] but this is an arguably short-sighted read of religious history. The distrust of reason when applied to the "things of God" did not begin with the Reformation. On the contrary, as history has shown, the Reformation was, arguably, *the* catalyst for the ascen-

43. Hooker, *Lawes* 5.67. Ellrodt quotes the end of this passage in his proof, though he incorrectly ascribes it to *Lawes* 5.57.

44. See in particular Donne's Whitsunday sermon (1630?): "When the Church fell upon the *Quomodo* in the Sacrament, How, in what manner the body of Christ was there, we see what an inconvenient answer it fell upon, That it was done by Transubstantiation; That satisfied not, (as there was no reason it should) And then they fell upon others, *In, Sub,* and *Cum,* and none could, none can give satisfaction." In *The Sermons of John Donne,* ed. George R. Potter and Evelyn M. Simpson, 10 vols. (Berkeley: University of California Press, 1953–62), 9:246.

45. Hooker, *Lawes,* 5.57.

46. Strier, "George Herbert and Ironic Ekphrasis," 98.

dancy of reason and ingenuity.[47] Erasmus's biblical scholarship, which concentrates more on linguistics and hermeneutics than theology and the encounter with the divine,[48] and Descartes's *cogito*, which bifurcates creation into two isolated spheres, are only two examples of how such a movement infiltrated the minds of even ostensibly Catholic thinkers. Herbert, rather than exhibiting an anti-intellectual, Reform-minded anxiety, draws on the ancient Christian trust in faith over reason when it comes to questions of God. The Christian tradition inherited by Herbert surely held reason in esteem, but, the centrality of the Christian message resides in trust in the revealed mystery of Christ, "unto the Jews a stumbling block, and unto the Greeks foolishness" (1 Cor 1:23).

The Eucharist is central to Herbert's spirituality because it is the most immediately accessible, *physical* contact with Christ, and, therefore, the most readily attainable encounter with grace, even more than scripture, as he writes in the final stanza of "Peace,"

> Take of this grain, which in my garden grows,
> And grows for you;
> Make bread of it; and that repose
> And peace, which ev'ry where
> With so much earnestnesse you do pursue,
> Is onely there. (37–42)

The operative term here is "onely." Herbert visits this idea in several other poems. In "Divinitie," for instance, he writes

> But he doth bid us take his bloud for wine.
> Bid what he please; yet I am sure,
> To take and taste what he doth designe,
> Is all that saves, and not obscure. (25–29)

---

47. A considerable scholarly literature exists on this subject. See, in particular, Marcel Gauchet, *The Disenchantment of the World: A Political History of Religion*, trans. Oscar Burge (Princeton: Princeton University Press, 1999); Charles Taylor, *A Secular Age* (Cambridge: Belknap-Harvard University Press, 2007); and Brad Gregory, *The Unintended Reformation: How a Religious Revolution Secularized Society* (Cambridge: Belknap-Harvard University Press, 2012).

48. Albert Rabil, Jr., *Erasmus and the New Testament: The Mind of a Christian Humanist* (San Antonio, TX: Trinity University Press, 1972), especially 58–61.

Here he reemphasizes the "onely" proposition of "Peace" by asserting that the Eucharistic blood—mystically and actually identical with Christ's blood poured out at the Passion—"Is all that saves." Herbert also presents the Eucharist as central to Christian life in "An Offering," "The Bunch of Grapes," "Divinitie," "The Priesthood," and "The Banquet," but perhaps nowhere as poignantly as in "The Collar" and "Love (III)."

In "The Collar," in the midst of the speaker's full-blown despair and resultant rejection of his vocation as a priest, Herbert gives us a perversion of the Eucharist, an idea anticipated from the poem's first line "I Struck the board, and cry'd, No more," the "board," as many (but by no means all) have argued, indicating the Communion Table.[49] The poem's Eucharist is perverted because the speaker perverts his vocation by his insistence on escaping God's will:

> Sure there was wine
> Before my sighs did drie it: there was corn
> Before my tears did drown it. (10–12)

The speaker's rage and blasphemy turn the Eucharistic elements to their opposites. Wine is not dry: bread (corn) is; bread, dry by nature, is destroyed by immersion in water. The speaker, then, by his disobedience has metaphorically inverted and destroyed the Eucharist. Herbert's speaker could have rebelled against anything— scripture, ecclesia, ceremony—but he explicitly rebels against the priesthood as it relates to the Eucharist. Obviously, for Herbert the priesthood exists *because* of the Eucharist. Julia Carolyn Guernsey argues that in the poem Herbert imagines a speaker trying "to free himself from the constraints of religious life,"[50] which is surely correct, but it is even more due to the fact that, for Herbert, the religious life of the priest centers upon the Eucharist. Herbert himself affirms this notion in "The Priesthood":

49. Nevertheless, Herbert's statement in "Conscience," cited earlier, makes a pretty serious claim that the board of "The Collar" is, indeed, the Communion Table: "when ever at his *board* / I do but taste it, straight it cleanseth me" (14–15). My emphasis.

50. Julia Carolyn Guernsey, *The Pulse of Praise: Form as a Second Self in the Poetry of George Herbert* (Cranbury, NJ: Associated University Presses, 1999), 103.

But th' holy men of God such vessels are,
As serve him up, who all the world commands:
When God vouchsafeth to become our fare,
Their hands convey him, who conveys their hands.
O what pure things, most pure must those things be,
Who bring my God to me! (25–30)

The antimetabole "Their hands convey him, who conveys their hands" directly speaks the reciprocal and paradoxical phenomenon of consecration. Indeed, according to the poem, the priest holding a chalice—a "vessel"—is himself a vessel in the hands of God. Clearly, the priesthood, for Herbert, is unthinkable apart from the Eucharist.

Herbert's ultimate statement on the Eucharist arrives with the final poem of *The Church*. In "Love (III)," a particularly affective poetic moment concludes a shorter sequence that begins with "Death" and proceeds through "Dooms-day," "Judgement," and "Heaven." This short sequence (the "long sequence," indeed, begins with the vision of the Communion Table provided by "The Altar") serves as an imaginative account of the "Last Things," the events leading through death and to the Beatific Vision.

"Love (III)" is Herbert's take on the Beatific Vision, and, in keeping with his attention to enstatic as opposed to ecstatic religious experience, it is a low-key, modestly drawn picture of the encounter with God. It is also highly Eucharistic. The poem takes place in heaven, following the speaker's death. *The Temple*, then, ends in heaven with a Eucharistic celebration—just as *The Church* begins with anticipation of the earthly Eucharist intrinsic to "The Altar."[51] Bloch argues that the poem is not meant to take place in heaven, but that it is simply a Communion poem.[52] Such a view certainly problematizes our reading of the poem, but many readers will find this

51. As with many other scholars, I have serious doubts about whether Herbert thought of *The Church Militant* as the collection's coda. Its placement, in fact, spoils the religious aesthetic built throughout the work. It may work as an appendix, but not as a final word. I find myself in agreement with Martz who writes that the poem, "in many respects, may seem to represent a rather desperate effort to salvage, if only by way of appendix, a very early poem." See *Poetry of Meditation*, 289.
52. Bloch, *Spelling the Word*, 101.

difficult to accept in view of its placement.[53] Michael Schoenfeldt, for his part, tries to politicize Herbert's Beatific Vision by raising the Puritan/Anglican question about the proper posture for the reception of Communion, sitting or standing.[54] But, as Regina Schwartz has observed, the communion that takes place here is neither one informed by theological debate nor by scholastic definitions of terms and species.[55] Indeed, locating a theological or political debate in "Love (III)," I think, is to misread the poem entirely. Theology abides in rationalizing or explaining the *mysterion*, whereas in this poem and, arguably, throughout *The Temple*, Herbert is more interested the ways faith and the action of grace afford the believer the opportunity to transcend theological debate and enter into the *mysterion* itself. In heaven theological debate is superfluous, since, at that point, believing Christians will see God "face to face" and know him even as they are known (1 Cor 13:12). What we have instead of a political problem or a theological debate in the poem, then, is a picture of intimacy.

Feelings of inadequacy as yet burden the speaker, an example of what Arnold Stein has called "the human reluctance to accept love as a gift entire" in Herbert's poetry.[56] And because he is still preoccupied with ego-centric notions (the emphasis on "I") that he should somehow merit his Master's friendship, the speaker receives a gentle reprimand from Christ: "Who made the eyes but I?"[57] Indeed, Christ erases questions of inadequacy or merit, Herbert subtly argues in the poem, exactly as he erases doctrinal and theological distinctions in a heavenly Eucharist that figures a moment of homey comfort and a very real, very permanent Sabbath of rest.

---

53. She is aware that the sequence speaks against her, writing that the poem "does not entirely belong to this sequence of impersonal eschatological poems (though it gains in complexity if we read it with the sequence in mind)" (*Spelling the Word*, 101). Clearly, Herbert *wants* us to read it with the sequence in mind.

54. Schoenfeldt, *Prayer and Power*, 225.

55. Schwartz, *Sacramental Poetics*, 135.

56. Arnold Stein, *George Herbert's Lyrics* (Baltimore, MD: The Johns Hopkins University Press, 1968), 194.

57. With the exquisite paronomasia on "I"s and "eyes."

What "Love (III)" articulates even above Herbert's affection for the Eucharist is his trust in the presence of Christ in the Eucharist, and which, as *The Temple* illustrates, is synonymous with his presence in the Church, as well. The drama that unfolds throughout *The Temple*, then, is a drama of a Christian coming to terms with Christ's presence, or, rather, with the gift of Christ's presence. As Jean-Luc Marion describes it,

> The presence of Christ, and therefore also that of the Father, discloses itself by a gift: it can therefore be recognized only by a blessing. A presence, which gives itself by grace and identifies itself with this gift, can therefore be seen only in being received, and received only in being blessed.[58]

Throughout *The Temple*, Herbert repeatedly investigates the Christian life as it unfolds in the existential, mystical, and, above all, sacramental phenomenology of grace, and this grace always arrives in the form of a gift: as insight; as the still, small voice; and, most reliably, in the Eucharist, all of which attest to the ways in which a phenomenological attention to presence opens to immanence.[59] George Herbert's poetry, indeed, opens itself to immanence and, as a result, distances itself from a Calvinist over-emphasis on God's absolute transcendence.

As I have been arguing, Herbert traces the phenomenology of grace throughout the poems than comprise *The Temple*, leading his readers in a return to the primacy of a Christian religious experience that both transcends and, in its own way, corrects the theological. For Herbert, the primacy of the Christian religious experience unfolds in movements of grace: in moments of surprise or insight, in the audition of the "still, small voice," in the Eucharist. And these moments appear in the poetry not for the speaker (or poet) alone. They can also manifest in the experience of the reader. Indeed, one of the many wonderful things about *The Temple* is the way Herbert provides his readers with a phenomenology of grace that also

---

58. Jean-Luc Marion, *Prolegomena to Charity*, 129.
59. Adam Miller, *Badiou, Marion and St. Paul: Immanent Grace*, Continuum Studies in Continental Philosophy (London: Continuum, 2008), 65.

potentially enacts for them an experience of grace, a site of "double intentionality."

Sincere attention to an artifact, a work of art, a poem, a passage of scripture not infrequently results in a double intentionality, an opening to immanence, or perhaps to a "transcendent immanence," an oxymoron providing what may be the best approximation for describing such an event. George Herbert's poetry inhabits just such a space, exploring its permutations and possibilities and, even, experimenting with its practical applications. As mentioned earlier, Simone Weil's deep attention to Herbert's poem—even in translation—brought her to an encounter that surely would have pleased the seventeenth-century Anglican pastor: an awareness of the presence of Christ. Certainly, not every reader of Herbert has an experience along the likes of Weil's. But neither, I think, can she be the only one who has.

Robert Herrick, Little Gidding, and Spectres of an Old Religion

If you came this way in may time, you would find the hedges
White again, in May, with voluptuous sweetness.[1]

IT IS probably an understatement to say that by the seventeenth-century, the English Reformation had actualized a level of cultural schizophrenia utterly unanticipated by its sixteenth-century architects. The sixteenth-century, to be sure, had no lack of cultural insanity: the Dissolution of the Monasteries, the imposition of the Prayer Book, the destruction of the altars, the rejection of the Mass, to say nothing of the human costs of reform, all emphatically enunciated the physical and collateral effects of the New English World Order—the total and irreversible destruction of over a thousand years of a unified cultural sensibility and identity. But, by the time of the disruption known as the Civil War, Reformation had turned on itself in the realization of the "rage for reform" that had been lurking beneath the surface of Western Christendom from at least the realist-nominalist debates of the medieval period. It is not without cause, then, that the English early modern period has been called the era of "the English Reformations."[2] Indeed, the reforms kept on coming. Though Protestantism had soundly won the day in England by the reign of Elizabeth I, during the first decades of the seventeenth century many of the reformed were suspected of not being quite reformed enough, and were often accused of "popish" sentiments and a lack of appropriate zeal. Then, with ascendancy of the Puritan Parliamentarians, the anti-Catholic hysteria of the pre-

---

1. T. S. Eliot, "Little Gidding" from *Four Quartets*, lines 24–25.
2. Christopher Haigh, *English Reformations: Religion, Politics and Society under the Tudors* (Oxford: The Clarendon Press, 1993).

vious century reincarnated in an existential manifestation of *l'éter-nel retour* as the persecution of Anglican Royalists aimed at Catholics in the previous century. This return was rendered all the more emblematic in the execution (some have said martyrdom) of King Charles I on 30 January 1649, an event which presaged James II's deposition during what has been called "the Glorious Revolution," at least according to the Whig metanarrative: another mile marker in "England's prolonged, patchy, and political Reformation."[3] But, I am not altogether convinced that the English religious reformation has finished. Even now. When it comes to the human preoccupation with reform, there is certainly some truth in the notion that "the world [is] a circular movement that has already repeated itself infinitely often and plays its game *ad infinitum.*"[4]

The Puritan "soft pogrom," then, the actualization of the desire for a totalizing reform aimed at Anglican intractability, evoked the spectre of the anti-Catholic attitudes (and policies) characteristic of the reigns of the Tudors Henry, Edward, and Elizabeth, as well of those of the first Stuart monarch, James I—especially after the Gunpowder Plot turned anti-Catholicism into a *de facto* article of British religion and cultural identity. This rage for order was in resonance with an ethos Mary Midgley has identified as simultaneously occurring in the context of the scientific revolution: a cultural development which also "displayed a new purifying zeal, a passion for disinfection, at times a cognitive washing-compulsion, accompanied by a rather touching willingness to accept a minor role in the great cleansing process."[5] Even if in a negative manner, the Catholic spectre continued to maintain a formidable presence in the English cultural imaginary.

In this chapter I will argue that the Catholic spectre also persisted in more affirmative manifestations which were primarily commu-

3. Alexandra Walsham, *Providence in Early Modern England* (Oxford: Oxford University Press, 1999), 328.

4. Friedrich Nietzsche, *The Will to Power*, trans. J.M. Kennedy, ed. Oscar Levy, vol. 9 of *The Complete Works of Friedrich Nietzsche* (Edinburgh: T.N. Foulis, 1913), 430.

5. Mary Midgley, *Science as Salvation: A Modern Myth and Its Meaning* (London: Routledge, 1992), 79.

nitarian in nature, though this communitarianism was inseparable from both religious and folk cultural forms and practices both persisting and transmogrifying through the period—the anxieties of which were troubled by not only the Puritan ascendancy but also by economic pressures (such as enclosure laws) that by degrees had long been compromising nascent English communitarianism by economic accretion, an instrumentalization of the commons that has been called "a revolution of the rich against the poor."[6] In particular, I will focus on the ways this phenomenon appears in Robert Herrick's poetry and in the experiment in Christian living undertaken by Nicholas Ferrar and his family at Little Gidding.

Robert Herrick

Herrick's poetry, for all its deceptive simplicity, is as complicated as life. As scholars beginning with John L. Kimmey in the 1970s have recognized, one aspect of Herrick's aesthetic is to celebrate the "delight in disorder" that is nowhere more evident than in the arrangement (or seeming lack of arrangement) in *Hesperides* and the appended *Noble Numbers*.[7] In the construction of his book, Herrick seems to suffer from poetic ADHD: he apparently flits from the persona of that of flirtatious rapscallion to skewering Martialian epigrammatist, from Roman pagan offering oblations to the lares to the Devonshire vates memorializing the resilient folk religion and Catholic past of his parish. It is has been argued that the prevailing structure (if that is indeed the word) of *Hesperides* is characterized by the way "one poem undermines another and dispels its aura of aesthetic perfection."[8] My contention is that Herrick's disordered order and apparent self-subversion disclose an aesthetic that has as its theme the depiction of actual life. Herrick, then, is a realist: he shows life as it is lived, the human personality as it really operates, human community in its manifold functions and dysfunctions.

6. Karl Polanyi, *The Great Transformation* (Boston: Beacon Press, 1957), 35.

7. John L. Kimmey, "Order and Form in Herrick's *Hesperides*," *The Journal of English and Germanic Philology* 70, no. 1 (April 1971): 255–68.

8. Leah S. Marcus, "Conviviality Interrupted or, Herrick and Postmodernism" in *Lords of Wine and Oil*, 65–82, at 70.

Sometimes, as critics have noticed, he loves the country; sometimes he hates it.[9] Sometimes he loves his neighbors; sometimes he loathes them. Academics, so often compromised by the politics of their profession, sometimes have a hard time understanding that actual human life, lived for the most part by people outside of the academy, is not a constant pitting of allegiances, a never-ending game of Darwinian survival of the fittest mixed with acquiescence to the will of the egregore. Herrick's poetry and its arrangement have to be messy because life is: not because he's unstable or hasn't figured out where he stands. He knows where he stands: in chaos.

Among a variety of ways, Herrick counters his historical moment with the ordered disorder of his verse through his placement of the English Catholic past into his own troubled Protestant present in the constructed world of *Hesperides*, creating a "Poetick Liturgie"[10] that celebrates every facet of a rapidly disappearing, if not already vanished, notion of human flourishing: a world rapidly decaying into the archipelago of citizen-states characteristic of secularization. His collection, then, stands both as a monument and as a dirge which laments the passing of an age. Indeed, Herrick recognizes his own inclusion in such a phenomenon in his book's frontispiece, which imagines a monument to himself, and in the many poems in which he anticipates his own demise.

Herrick, first of all, includes numerous images and ideas which explicitly invoke England's Catholic past. Herrick employs the term "Matins," for example (usually spelled "Mattens"), enough to raise some Puritan eyebrows in "To the Lark" (H-214), "To Julia" (H-1069), and, especially, in the wryly titled "Mattens, or Morning Prayer" (H-320). Matins, the Catholic morning service, was transformed by the architects of the English Reformation into "Morning Prayer," and was institutionalized by its inclusion in the *Book of*

9. Jessica Tvordi, "The Poet in Exile: Robert Herrick and the 'loathed Country-life'" in *Rural Space in the Middle Ages and Early Modern Age: The Spatial Turn in Pre-Modern Studies*, ed. Albrecht Classen with collaboration of Christopher R. Clason (Berlin: De Gruyter, 2012), 795–818, at 808.

10. Robert Herrick, "To His Kinswoman, Mistresse Penelope Wheeler" [H-510], line 4. From *The Complete Poetry of Robert Herrick*, ed. J. Max Patrick (New York: Norton, 1968). All quotations from Herrick are from this edition.

Common Prayer. In the 1549 edition of the Prayer Book, the service is called "Matynns," whereas the in 1559 edition the service is entitled "An Order for Morning Prayer Daily throughout the Year," though in the index of "Proper Lessons to Be Read for the First Lessons Both at Morning Prayer and Evening Prayer…" the name "Matins" is used. Some of the more zealous Puritans even took issue with the term "Morning Prayer" which, after their rise to power, in 1645 they wished changed to "Morning Exercise."[11] Though, in general, those of a more extreme Puritan bent despised the prayer book as tainted by popishness, and some even conjectured that it was "the invention of the pope of Rome."[12] Herrick was fully aware of the charged rhetorical fray into which he was entering, and he further pushed the bounds of Puritan toleration by adding to his poetic lexicon references to "incense" (e.g., "To the Lark," line 15, among many others), "Holy-water," and "Beads" ("To Julia," lines 5 and 7), as well as the notion of "Crossing thy selfe" mentioned in "Mattens, or Morning Prayer" (line 2). The images of crossing and beads (as in the Rosary), in particular, would have created concern even among a good many Anglicans. Herrick was well aware of this: and he uses such references to Catholic methods of prayer repeatedly in order to poke his finger into the eye of the Puritan establishment.[13] Another explicitly Catholic image Herrick turns to upon occasion is a figure emblematic of Catholicism for early modern (and postmodern) Protestants: the Virgin Mary.

The first explicit reference to the Virgin occurs in *Hesperides* when, in the poem "To Julia, in her Dawn, or Day-breake," Herrick writes:

> By the next kindling of the day
> My *Julia* thou shalt see,

11. Richard Davey, *The Pageant of London, Volume 2: AD 1500 to 1900* (London: Methuen & Co., 1906), 240.

12. Essex Record Office assize files, 35/84: 1641/13. Quoted in Brian Cummings (ed.), *The Book of Common Prayer: The Texts of 1549, 1559, and 1662* (Oxford; Oxford University Press, 2011), notes to Morning Prayer, 757.

13. In, for example, "Corinna's gone a Maying" (H-178, line 27), "Pray and Prosper" (H370, line 2), "Crutches" (H-973, line 7), and "To his peculiar friend Master John Wicks" (H-1056, line 16), among others.

> Ere *Ave-Mary* thou canst say
> Ile come and visit thee. (lines 1–4)

In the allusion to the Catholic prayer to the Virgin, framed in a contemporary (and not historical) context, Herrick implies a present reality: a prayer context still valid because still in use.

In *Noble Numbers* Herrick's three poems on the Virgin Mary further assert a Catholic sensibility. The Marian poems are quite straightforward, but they are not without subtle elements of Herrickian humor and provocation:

The Virgin Mary [N-183]

> To work a *wonder*, God would have her shown,
> At once, a Bud, and yet a *Rose full-blowne.*

Another [N-184]

> As Sun-beames pierce the glasse, and streaming in,
> No crack or Schisme leave i'th subtill skin:
> So the Divine Hand work't, and brake no thred,
> But, in a *Mother*, kept a *maiden-head.*

The Virgin Mary [N-190]

> The *Virgin Marie* was (as I have read)
> The *House of God*, by *Christ* inhabited;
> Into the which He enter'd: but, the Doore
> Once shut, was never to be open'd more.

Certainly, Herrick's Marian poems cannot be construed as explicitly or overtly Catholic, and most Anglicans of his time would have found little in them with which to argue. But Puritans were a different story, and it is with them in mind that the militancy of Herrick's Marian poems needs to be contextualized. Typical of Puritan divines, Richard Baxter dismissed, among other Catholic devotional practices, "dropping Beads, praying to the Virgin *Mary*, and to other Saints" as altogether irrational religious practices that "do most heinously dishonour God."[14] As Christina Luckyj has observed, some

---

14. Richard Baxter, *A Christian Directory or Body of Practical Divinity* (London, 1677), 150.

Puritans projected their Marian anxieties onto the Catholic Church in ways that would have delighted Freud.[15] Horrified by the valuation of the feminine in Catholicism, the newly Protestant Sir Anthony Hungerford writes to his own Catholic mother of the feminized Catholic Church: "Shee that teacheth us to pray to God, wil command us likewise to pray *to our blessed Ladie, and the Saints*" and he also complains of the teaching that "our selves must make satisfaction for some sort of our sins, by our workes of penance, the which if wee neglect, that then wee must satisfie Gods justice for them after this life by suffering paines in a purgatory fire, unlesse this holy Mother out of compassion shall free us by her indulgence."[16] Herrick, who had no problems either with women or the Virgin Mary, had been ejected from his living at Dean Prior in 1647 following the Puritan rise to power. He published *Hesperides* with *Noble Numbers* in 1648, and it is my contention that the implicit Catholicism in his collection is an explicit, if slightly cloaked, affront to the ruling powers of mid-century English politics and religion, the early modern equivalent of "Come at me, bro!" A similar development occurs between the two parts of Henry Vaughan's *Silex Scintillans*, published in installments in 1650 and 1655. Vaughan's 1655 addition is even more militantly Marian and implicitly Catholic as anything in Herrick's collection. Indeed, Vaughan makes sure his detractors won't miss his rhetorical challenge by placing it in the dedication to his 1655 edition:

> To my most merciful, my most
> loving, and dearly loved Re-
> deemer, the ever blessed,
> the onely Holy and
> JUST ONE,

---

15. Christina Luckyj, "Disciplining the Mother in Seventeenth-Century English Puritanism," in *Performing Maternity in Early Modern England*, ed. Kathryn M. Moncrief and Kathryn R. McPherson, Studies in Performance and Early Modern Drama (Aldershot, UK: Ashgate, 2007), 101–14, at 107–08.

16. Anthony Hungerford, *The Advise of a Sonne, Now Professing the Religion Established in the present Church of England, to his deare Mother, yet a Roman Catholike* (Oxford, 1616), 8–9. Italics in source.

JESUS CHRIST,
The Son of the living
GOD,
And the sacred
Virgin Mary.[17]

It comes as no surprise that Vaughan, too, was a Royalist, and that in the interim between the publication of the two parts of *Silex* his twin brother, the Anglican priest and natural philosopher Thomas Vaughan, had been ejected from his living at Llansantffraid (St. Bridget's parish) in Brecon, Wales after the *Act for better Propagation and Preaching the Gospel in Wales* was proclaimed in 1650.[18] Herrick, like Vaughan, knew there were weapons just as useful as steel and powder in the battle for England.

In addition to the more easily detectable Catholic ideas in his work, Herrick also includes poems of a more subtle Catholic sensibility in *Hesperides*. One example of this implicit Catholicism occurs in the collection by way of metaphor: in the numerous poems that pay homage to the lares, the household gods of ancient Rome, and the evocations of Herrick's poetic persona as a "Roman citizen."

In ancient Rome, the lares (often associated with the penates) were understood as "part and parcel of the life of the home, and their little statues might be seen decorated with miniature garlands of flowers on special occasions."[19] In Roman antiquity, they were often, though not exclusively, understood to be the deceased members of the family, as is implied in *Aeneid* 1.69, wherein Virgil describes Aeneas as *"Ilium in Italiam portans victosque Penates,"* *"bearing Ilium and his defeated household gods into Italy."* And, in fact, Virgil's most frequent epithet for his hero is *"pius Aeneas,"*

---

17. *The Complete Poetry of Henry Vaughan*, ed. French Fogle, The Stuart Editions (New York: New York University Press, 1965), 264.

18. For more on the Vaughans' Marian sensibilities, see the chapter entitled "The Rosicrucian Mysticism of Henry and Thomas Vaughan" in Michael Martin, *Literature and the Encounter with God in Post-Reformation England* (Farnham, UK: Ashgate, 2014).

19. "Religious Practices of the Home and the Family: Rome" in *Religions of the Ancient World: A Guide,* Sarah Iles Johnston, general ed. (Cambridge: Harvard University Press, 2004), 435–36, at 436.

"pious Aeneas," a testament as much to his devotion to his family and ancestors as it is to his respect for the gods: all qualities Herrick emphasizes in his self-characterizations in *Hesperides* and *Noble Numbers*.

Herrick mentions the lares repeatedly in his poetry, as early as "His Sailing from Julia" [H-35], where he writes, "Devoutly to thy *Closet-gods* then pray, / That my wing'd ship may meet no *Remora*" (lines 3–4). Like Aeneas, Herrick's alter-ego speaker in the poem "To his Household gods" carries his lares with him as he embarks for Devonshire from his native and beloved London:

> Rise, Household-gods, and let us goe;
> But whither, I my selfe not know.
> First, let us dwell on rudest seas;
> Next, with severest Salvages;
> Last, let us make our best abode,
> Where humane foot, as yet, ne'er trod:
> Search worlds of Ice; and rather there
> Dwell, then in lothed *Devonshire*. (H-278)

While some have attempted to depict poems like this in the context of an assumed "rural loathing" on Herrick's part, it would be wrong to conclude that such was Herrick's consistent attitude.[20] Indeed, disdain for exile or occasional disgust with one's geographical setting are common human sentiments, and one wonders whether scholarly sympathy with Herrick's exile from London might tell us more about a critic writing from an office in rural Tennessee or Nebraska than about a Londoner poet writing from Devonshire.

Indeed, Herrick celebrates the lares even in Dean Prior:

> At my homely Country-seat,
> I have there a little wheat;
> Which I worke to a Meale, and make
> Therewithall a *Holy-cake*:
> Part of which I give to *Larr*,
> Part is my peculiar.
> ("Larr's portion, and the Poets part" [H-392])

---

20. Jessica Tvordi, "The Poet in Exile," 812–17.

His poems to the lares may evoke the Roman pagan past that so many of his critics rejoice in as it, they think, discards the cumbersome apparatus of Christianity; but Herrick is a more subtle poet than they give him credit for. The lares may be household gods, but they are also—even for Romans—ancestors.

My claim is that Herrick's treatment of the lares in his poetry poeticizes (and disguises) another kind of "Roman" sensibility. In "The Primitiæ to Parents," then, Herrick discloses a deeper layer of the lares motif:

> Our *Household-gods* our Parents be;
> And manners good requires, that we
> The first Fruits give to them, who gave
> Us hands to get what here we have. (H-647)

The dead are certainly not inaccessible in Herrick's theology. In opposition to the Puritan thought of his day, the notions of the Communion of Saints—especially in the sense of a viable commerce between the living and the dead, among other things—and the efficacy of prayers to the deceased ring loud and clear in Herrick. These very Catholic ideas were habitually maligned in Puritan preaching and pamphlets of the age: "We cannot help the Dead by praying for them, nor can they hear us when we pray unto them. Yea, the Popish Religion is not only ridiculous, but Idolatrous."[21] Fortunately for the world of English poetry, Herrick was never one to fear being thought ridiculous.

This reciprocity between the physical and spiritual realms is important for Herrick and he nowhere so clearly articulates it as in a poem with unmistakably Catholic overtones, "Purgatory":

> Readers wee ent[r]eat ye pray
> For the soule of *Lucia*;
> That in little time she be
> From her *Purgatory* free:

---

21. "Sermon XV: Invocation of Saints and Angels, unlawful" in *The Morning-Exercise against Popery. or, the Principal Errors of the Church of Rome Detected and Confuted in a Morning-Lecture Preached lately in Southwark: by Several Ministers of the Gospel in or near London* (London, 1675), 547.

In th'*intrim* she desires
That your teares may coole her fires. (H-814)

Tellingly, the critical commentary on the poem is essentially non-existent, limited to only a passing mention of it by Achsah Guibbory in a broader discussion of Herrick's sympathies for some of the more Catholic elements of Laud's reform of the reform.[22] If nothing else, the poem casts more than a hockcart-full of doubt on the all-too-numerous assertions that Herrick was really a closet Roman pagan in the sense of Ovidian *antiqua religione*.[23]

In evoking the idea of Purgatory, Herrick not only thumbs his nose at Puritan precisians, but simultaneously distances himself from the theology of Archbishop William Laud, even though Herrick was in many, many ways ("too many to be coincidental"[24]) in agreement with him. Laud was in favor of prayers for the dead, but rejected the notion of Purgatory. Recapitulating his dispute with Robert Bellarmine on the issue, Laud criticizes the Jesuit theologian's claim that the Fathers "affirm *Prayer for the dead*, as if that must necessarily infer *Purgatory*. Whereas most certain it is, that the *Ancients* had, and gave other Reasons of *Prayer for the dead*, then freeing them out of any *Purgatory*."[25] Laud's performance here left enough ambiguity for Puritans to accuse him of "popishness," and he felt compelled to defend himself from that charge (and others) prior to his execution at their hands in 1645.[26] As Peter Marshall has

---

22. Achsah Guibbory, *Ceremony and Community from Herbert to Milton: Literature, Religion, and Cultural Conflict in Seventeenth-Century England* (Cambridge: Cambridge University Press, 1998), 91.

23. See L. C. Martin's commentary in his edition of *The Poetical Work of Robert Herrick* (Oxford: The Clarendon Press, 1956), 567. This is also the center of H. R. Swardson's discussion of Herrick in the chapter entitled "Herrick and the Ceremony of Mirth" in his *Poetry and the Fountain of Light: Observations on the Conflict between Christian and Classical Traditions in Seventeenth-Century Poetry* (Columbia: University of Missouri Press, 1962), 40–63.

24. Achsah Guibbory, *Ceremony and Community from Herbert to Milton*, 89.

25. *A Relation of the Conference between William Laud, Late Lord Arch-bishop of Canterbury, and Mr. Fisher the Jesuit, by Command of King James, of ever Blessed Memory*, 4th ed. (London, 1685/6), 227.

26. In Laud's *apologia* he writes: "This 'treason in the altitude,' he said, was in my endeavour to alter the religion established by law, and to subvert the laws

noted, earlier during the English Reformation the notion that *preces pro defunctis non supponunt purgatorium* ("prayers for the dead did not suppose Purgatory") "was a commonplace of Elizabethan and Jacobean anti-Catholic polemic," but by the time of the Civil War recommending prayers for the deceased "had come to be seen as an invitation to popish apostasy."[27] Herrick, rather than distancing himself from such popish customs, instead embraces them. In his book-length meditation on the subject, Stephen Greenblatt recognizes in the "brilliance of the doctrine of Purgatory" complementary matters of "institutional control over ineradicable folk beliefs and . . . engagement with intimate, private feelings"[28]—notions at least partially compatible with Herrick's poetic treatment of the topic. But even more than his allusions to the Catholic past— whether direct as in the cases of beads and Purgatory, or indirect as in the case of the household gods—Herrick's innate Catholic sensibilities show themselves in his many poems celebrating folk life and ritual tied to both the agricultural and the Christian years.

The critical history of Herrick's folk religion embodies all of the problems of the religious nature of his verse. Is it Roman pagan? Nostalgically Catholic? Laudian Anglican? Does Herrick celebrate folk customs in his verse that he observed in his Devonshire parish? Or is he celebrating the Caroline court's dilettantish and performative appropriation of all things pastoral? The real problem, I think,

---

themselves; and that to effect these I left no way unattempted. For religion, he told the Lords, that I laboured a reconciliation with Rome; that I maintained Popish and Arminian opinions; that I suffered transubstantiation, justification by merits, purgatory, and what not, to be openly preached all over the kingdom; that I induced superstitious ceremonies, as consecrations of churches and chalices, and pictures of Christ in glass windows; that I gave liberty to the profanation of the Lord's day; that I held intelligence with cardinals and priests, and endeavoured to ascend to papal dignity,—offers being made to me to be a cardinal." From *The Works of the Most Reverend Father in God, William Laud, D.D., sometime Lord Archbishop of Canterbury: Volume IV: History of Troubles and Trial, &c.* (Oxford: John Henry Parker, 1854), 55–56.

27. Peter Marshall, *Beliefs and the Dead in Reformation England* (Oxford: Oxford University Press, 2002), 186.

28. Stephen Greenblatt, *Hamlet in Purgatory* (Princeton: Princeton University Press, 2001), 102.

is in trying to pin Herrick down to a particular faction. His vision of Christianity is bigger than that—but it doesn't include everyone. In particular, Herrick's evocation of a communitarian spirit in his verse challenges the Puritan sourpusses who not only disliked feasting and frolic but wanted to—and eventually did— create laws that did their best to eradicate any and all delights connected to the Christian year. As Shakespeare's Sir Toby Belch tells the pompous Puritan Malvolio in *Twelfth Night*: "Dost thou think, because thou art virtuous, there shall be no more cakes and ale?"[29] Many precisians, indeed, attempted to curtail the enjoyment of cakes and ale connected with merrymaking. Upon coming into power they erased as much merriment from the English year as possible— including the removal of Christmas as a Christian feast and holy day, which ruined in its wake the merry season between Christmas and Twelfth Night and also brought down maypoles and church ales in a ghastly resurgence of the same ethos inherent to the Visitation of the Monasteries in the sixteenth century.[30] Ultimately, "upon 10 June 1647 Christmas, Easter, Whitsun, and all other Church feasts ceased to exist in England by both secular law and ecclesiastical ruling."[31] (It was in 1647, of course, that Herrick was ejected from his living at Dean Prior.) Puritans not only disliked these things because of their own anxieties about merriment: they especially hated them because they believed these observances to be "popish" and full of superstition.

Connecting merriment to Catholicism—and thereby to the worst sort of paganism—had become a pretty standard Puritan trope by the mid-seventeenth century. The Puritan controversialist Thomas Hall (1610–1665) plays on this theme in *Funebria Floræ* (published in three editions, 1660–1661). His zealous vitriol is patent:

29. From *The Riverside Shakespeare,* ed. G. Blakemore Evans and J.J.M. Tobin, 2nd ed. (Boston: Houghton Mifflin Company, 1997), 2.3.115–16.

30. Ronald Hutton, *The Rise and Fall of Merry England: The Ritual Year 1400–1700* (Oxford: Oxford University Press, 1996), 205–12.

31. Ronald Hutton, *The Rise and Fall of Merry England*, 212.

So that I would debauch a people, and draw them from God and his worship to superstition and Idolatry, I would take this course: I would open this gap to them, they should have *Floralia* and *Saturnalia*, they should have feast upon feast (as 'tis in Popery) they should have Wakes to prophane the Lords-day, they should have May-Games, and Christmas-revels, with dancing, drinking, whoring, potting, piping, gaming, till they were made dissolute, and fit to receive any superstition, and easily drawn to bee of any, or of no Religion: And this was the practice of the late *Prelates*, when they were bringing in Popery by the head and shoulders (as is made apparent to the world out of their own writings) they first caused the book of sports to bee read in all Churches for the prophaning of the Sabbath (a lesson that people can learn too fast without a book) that so they might fit the people the better for the swallowing of those superstitious innovations, which shortly after followed.[32]

One can imagine the prelate Robert Herrick responding—enthusiastically—with "A toast!" This is precisely the function of his poetry.

Herrick's poetry, of course, is widely acknowledged as celebrating the carnival aspects of folk and religious life, even to the point where some question his religious sincerity, as if Christianity were all about melancholy and self-abnegation and antithetical to fun and procreative activity.[33] It may be for some, but not for everyone. Certainly not for Herrick. Indeed, many a critic exemplifies the early modern Puritan enthusiasm for a joy-killing Christianity even when that critic happens to be an agnostic or atheist.

But the central feature of Herrick's festal tone rests in his reliance on ritual and its role in binding communities together. It is with this in mind that the ordered disorder of *Hesperides* needs to be

32. Thomas Hall, *Funebria Floræ, the Downfall of May-Games...* 3rd edition, corrected (London, 1661), 13–14.

33. This is the case with much earlier criticism, as with Swardson, for example, who writes of the poet that "we are dealing with a Christian poet who felt the sense of opposition between his poetry and his religion, as so many poets of Herrick's century did" (Swardson, *Poetry and the Fountain of Light*, 42). Such an assessment would probably have moved the poet to respond with an acerbic epigram. Creaser is in general agreement with Swardson. See his "Jocund his Muse was," 45ff.

considered. As the Tudor wholesale extermination of Catholicism had in the sixteenth century, during and after the Civil War the Puritan zeal for reforming the reform and abolishing even the least traces of what might be consider "popish" following Archbishop Laud's partial retrieval of tradition was, in essence, a project dedicated to the disruption of community, a program devoted to the "divide and conquer and demoralize" methodology which modern states have ever since utilized as a template for "best practices."

Many critics, of course, have already addressed Herrick's interest in community, and none so comprehensively as Achsah Guibbory. Certainly, some have called her assessment into question—all interpretation is, after all, contingent—but her argument bears up remarkably well after almost twenty years. And while I don't have much to add to add to Guibbory's masterful contextualization of Herrick's preoccupation with community, I do think it necessary to add a few thoughts in consideration of Herrick's worldview in the light of communitarianism.

The term "communitarianism" is, admittedly, more than a trifle anachronistic when applied to Herrick's historical moment. But, nonetheless, I think it an apt one. The social pressures applied by a mixture of a creeping nascent capitalism—which had concerned Thomas More in *Utopia*[34] during the reign of Henry VIII—and what could be called a kind of "soft totalitarianism" (exemplified by both the Tudor reforms and the reforms imposed by Parliament during and after the Civil War) awakened in Herrick the desire to (re)affirm the sacredness—sublime at times, ridiculous at others— of what was being lost. In this, Herrick's poetry has much to say to postmodern communitarianism.

---

34. "[E]ven some abbots though otherwise holy men, are not content with the old rents that the land yielded to their predecessors. Living in idleness and luxury, without doing any good to society, no longer satisfies them; they have to do positive evil. For they leave no land free for the plow: they enclose every acre for pasture; they destroy houses and abolish towns, keeping only the churches, and those for sheep barns.... So your island, which seemed especially fortunate in this matter, will be ruined by the crass avarice of a few." Thomas More, *Utopia*, trans. and ed. Robert M. Adams, revised, 2nd ed. Norton Critical Editions in the History of Ideas (New York: W. W. Norton & Company, 1992), 12–13.

Communitarianism asserts a strong critique of modernity, a modernity in its infancy when Herrick lived. And the poet was amazingly prescient in seeing where it would lead and what was in danger of being lost:

> Lost to moderns are the manifest answers to existential questions provided by embeddedness with kin, culture, and place. Lost are pre-modern certainties of everyday rituals and known obligations. Lost is the intrinsic value of work, the sacredness of object and place, the natural rhythms of day and season. Lost also are the intimacy and trust generated from repeated face-to-face interactions in a society in which relationships are dense and multi-stranded.[35]

These are the things Herrick simultaneously celebrates and mourns in his verse, as he does in the melancholy strains that complete the otherwise celebratory "Corinna's going a Maying" (H-178):

> And as a vapour, or a drop of raine
> Once lost, can ne'er be found againe:
>> So when or you or I are made
>> A fable, song, or fleeting shade;
>> All love, all liking, all delight
>> Lies drown'd with us in endlesse night.
> Then while time serves, and we are but decaying;
> Come, my *Corinna*, come, let's goe a Maying. (lines 63–70)

Herrick's uses of *carpe diem*, then, are not only warnings about a lost moment, but of a lost age.

Charles Taylor, for one, has emphasized the importance of *communitas* as an element of human flourishing seriously compromised by the various reform movements, by the Enlightenment, and by all that goes by the name of "modernity." *Communitas* is found in the sacred (liturgy, preaching, communal prayer, pilgrimage), in the profane (carnival in all of its manifestations) and where both meet and coalesce in the life of the parish: in religious festivals,

---

35. Charles Heying, "Autonomy vs. Solidarity: Liberal, Totalitarian and Communitarian Traditions," *Administrative Theory & Praxis* 21, no. 1 (March 1999): 39–50, at 40.

the "good magic" of blessings and sacramentals, and in the myriad ways in which the Church year intersects with the progression of the seasons and the agricultural cycle. *Communitas*, furthermore,

> is the intuition we all share that, beyond the way we relate to each other through our diversified coded roles, we also are a community of many-sided human beings, fundamentally equal, who are associated together. It is this underlying community which breaks out in moments of reversal or transgression, and which gives legitimacy to the power of the weak.[36]

Communitas, then, seeing that it encapsulates not only the variety of human affiliations in the living of life as well as in the liturgical and agricultural cycles, is a thoroughly cosmological reality. Though certainly not the intent, the Protestant Reformation effectively destroyed any integral *communitas*:

> Reform comes to be seen as a serious business, brooking no alternatives. There is no more separate sphere of the 'spiritual' where one may go to pursue a life of prayer outside the saeculum; and nor is there the other alternative, between order and anti-order, which Carnival represented. There is just this one relentless order of right thought and action, which must occupy all social and personal space.[37]

This is exactly what transpired during the Civil War and the zeal of such reform no doubt contributed significantly to Herrick's ejection from Dean Prior. He was not alone in being harmed by a rage for reformation. As Michael Walzer has observed, "Calvinist saintliness, after all, has scarred us all."[38]

Communitas is, more than obviously, central to Herrick's religion as well as his poetry. This is why his collection is such a mélange composed of acerbic epigrams, poems celebrating love and fertility, religious verse, poems of self-parody, epithalamion, eulogy, prayer. His collection is a body of work that, by his own admission, repre-

36. Charles Taylor, *A Secular Age* (Cambridge: Harvard/Belknap Press, 2007), 49.

37. Ibid., 266.

38. Michael Walzer, *The Revolution of the Saints: A Study in the Origins of Radical Politics* (Cambridge: Harvard University Press, 1965), vii.

sents a "mixt Religion. . . . Part Pagan, part Papisticall,"[39] comprised of Laudian Anglicanism, pre-Reformation English Catholicism, folk and fairy traditions, and pagan Rome: these are things that characterize *communitas*, what Taylor has called a "multi-speed religion" characteristic of pre-Reformation Catholicism. *Communitas* is not univocal, but multifarious, messy, teaming with life and variety. This is what Herrick represents and why his verse, both *Hesperides* and *Noble Numbers*, stands as such an achievement. This is also why his collection's disordered order could be arranged in no other way, and why he prefaces it with

The Argument of his Book

I Sing of *Brooks*, of *Blossomes, Birds*, and *Bowers*,
Of *April, May*, of *June*, and *July*-Flowers.
I sing of *May-poles, Hock-carts, Wassails, Wakes*,
Of *Bride-grooms, Brides*, and of their *Bridall-cakes*.
I write of *Youth*, of *Love*, and have *Accesse*
By these, to sing of cleanly-*Wantonnesse*.
I sing of *Dewes*, of *Raines*, and piece by piece
Of *Balme*, of *Oyle*, of *Spice*, and *Amber-gris*.
I sing of *Time's trans-shifting*; and I write
How *Roses* first came *Red*, and *Lillies White*.
I write of *Groves*, of *Twilights*, and I sing
The court of *Mab*, and of the *Fairie-King*.
I write of *Hell*; I sing (and ever shall)
Of *Heaven*, and hope to have it after all. (H-1)

Eliot famously dismissed Herrick as a "minor poet."[40] Eliot was able to diagnose the problem of modernity and its roots in the English religious and political reformations of the early modern period, but he could offer no cure other than a kind of vague allegiance to "tradition." Herrick, on the other hand, knew the real cure—the alliance of religious and folk cultures—though, through no fault of his own, his project failed as completely as Eliot's.

---

39. "The Fairie Temple: or, Oberons Chappell. Dedicated to Master John Merifield, Counsellor at Law" (H-223), lines 23 and 25.
40. In the essay "What Is Minor Poetry?" (1944). See T.S. Eliot, *On Poetry and Poets* (New York: Farrar, Straus & Giroux, 2009), 34–51, at 44.

Roger Scruton has argued that "liturgies of religion involve a conjuring of absent things, and an attempt to sanctify the life of the community by lifting it from the realm of nature and endowing it with a kind of reasoned necessity."[41] I think that, on the whole, Scruton is right, but would modify his notion by saying that liturgies of religion—and certainly of Catholicism and the kind of Catholicism present in Herrick—likewise lift up nature and the cycle of the year in an anaphoric gesture sanctifying all things, albeit for a temporary, if nevertheless kairotic, moment. Herrick's poetry, when seen in this light, itself becomes, in his words, a "Poetick Liturgie." That is, Herrick's vast, unwieldy collection of verse ambling across *Hesperides* and *Noble Numbers* discloses itself as inherently sacramental (in the sense of the apotheosis of the things of this world in the service of God) and as *a* sacramental, indeed, a kind of holy relic carried as a charm against the powers of evil, be they political, existential, or metaphysical.

Nicholas Ferrar and Little Gidding

An alternate Anglican attempt to maintain a grasp on a remnant of an aspect of English religious culture rapidly disappearing amidst an ethos of reformation can be seen in the community founded by Nicholas Ferrar and his mother, Mary Woodnoth Ferrar, at Little Gidding in 1626, the year in which Nicholas was ordained deacon.

The Little Gidding community consisted exclusively of members of the Ferrar family, men, women, and (many) children, altogether numbering about thirty. The intention of the founding was simple: the community would be dedicated to "the steady, rhythmic routine of prayer and worship and consecrated effort provided in the daily rule of the household."[42] Part of their prayer life consisted in a twenty-four hour vigil of prayer kept in "watches," and in their holy discipline the family would by turns recite the entire Psalter twice

41. Roger Scruton, *The Soul of the World* (Princeton: Princeton University Press, 2014), 193.
42. A.L. Maycock, *Nicholas Ferrar of Little Gidding* (1938; reprt. Grand Rapids, MI: William B. Eerdmans Publishing Company, 1980), 156.

from sunrise to sunrise.[43] In addition, the family was devoted to teaching religion to their own and the neighboring children, to recording their own discussions on religious and political topics in a series of dialogues (in what was called the "Little Academy"), and in preparing a number of exquisite "Story Books" recounting lives of the saints (both pre-Reformation and Protestant) as well as some likewise extraordinary harmonies of the gospels.[44] Indeed, it has been argued that the Ferrars were invested in an undertaking in which "the final aim [was] the revival of the Religious Life in the Church of England."[45] This revival was not without its critics.

When Edward Lenton visited the Little Gidding community in 1633 or 1634, he was somewhat alarmed at what he took to be the papistical practices of the Ferrars, though he was not unimpressed by their graciousness, and gave a full report of his observations in a letter to Sir Thomas Hetley. In 1641, following the Puritan rise to political dominance that unleashed a good deal of religious venom toward anything remotely smacking of Roman Catholicism, Lenton's letter was manipulated in order to malign the Ferrars in a hateful little pamphlet, *The Arminian Nunnery: or, a Briefe Description and Relation of the late erected Monasticall Place, called the Arminian Nunnery at Little Gidding in Huntington-Shire.*

Though it begins mildly (in keeping with Lenton's original tone) the pamphlet fairly oozes with zealous disparagement. The speaker, describing his alleged visit to Little Gidding and a discussion with Nicholas Ferrar, confesses his concern at some rumors about the community:

> I first told him what I had heard of the *Nunns* at *Gidding*; of *two watching and praying all night*; of their *Canonicall houres*; of their *Crosses* on the outside and inside of the *Chappell*; of an *Altar* richly decked with *Tapestry, Plate* and *Tapers*; of their *Adorations, genu-*

---

43. Ibid., 220.

44. The Story Books and harmonies were handmade and bound in sumptuous morocco bindings. Among others, George Herbert was the recipient of one of the harmonies as a gift. See Joyce Ransome, *The Web of Friendship: Nicholas Ferrar and Little Gidding* (London: James Clarke & Co., 2011), 69–70.

45. Bernard Blackstone, "Story Books of Little Gidding: Wine and Poetry," *The Times Literary Supplement* (21 March 1936): 238.

flections, and *geniculations,* which I told them plainly might strongly savour of Superstition and Popery.[46]

The speaker furthermore disparages Nicholas Ferrar as his "Priest-like pregnant Prolocutor" and calls into question the community's "new forme of *Fasting* and *Prayer,* and a contemplative idle life, a lip-labour devotion, and a will-worship . . . which by the word of God is no better than a specious idlenesse"[47]—all stock Puritan insults of Catholicism. The speaker is likewise scandalized that the Ferrars often employ the monogram "IHS" on their publications and as ornament of their chapel and house as they symbolize (to the jaundiced Puritan eye) "the proper Character of the Iesuites,"[48] apparently forgetting Constantine's vision of the Chi-Rho at the Milvian bridge, inscribed *Εν Τούτῳ Νικα (En toutō nika).*[49] He was not the only one scandalized: upon his visitation to the community in 1641 and seeing the IHS placed in the chapel, the Ferrars' bishop, John Williams, instructed Nicholas's brother John "to take this down, and let it not hang in this public room any longer."[50] The writer of *The Arminian Nunnery* is furthermore offended by the Ferrars' habit of bowing to sacred images, by their custom of beautifying the chapel with flowers, tapestries, a chalice and an altar, and he even takes issue with their ministry in "Physicke and Chirgurey."[51] But the biggest piece of papist heresy he finds is in the discipline adopted by Ferrar's nieces, Mary and Anna Collett, by which they were not only devoted to prayer and service, but also to lives of perpetual virginity. This, in his opinion, establishes Little Gidding as a nunnery, though Nicholas denied the charge:

---

46. *The Arminian Nunnery: or, a Briefe Description and Relation of the late erected Monasticall Place, called the Arminian Nunnery at Little Gidding in Hunting-ton-Shire* (1641), 2. Emphasis in text.

47. *The Arminian Nunnery,* 3–4.

48. Ibid., 5.

49. Throughout Christian history, Constantine's Greek has typically been translated into Latin as *in hoc signo vinces,* "in this sign conquer" and shortened to "IHS."

50. John Ferrar and Doctor Jebb, *Nicholas Ferrar: Two Lives* (Cambridge: Cambridge University Press, 1855), 72.

51. *The Arminian Nunnery,* 6–8.

He denied the place to be a *Nunnery*, and that none of his Neeces were *Nunnes*: but hee confessed that two of his *Nieces* had lived the one thirtie, the other thirty and two yeares Virgins, and so resolved to continue (as he hoped they would) to give themselves to *Fasting* and *Prayers*; but had made no *Vowes*.[52]

Such a discipline he finds reprehensible, since it makes the community

just like as the English *Nunnes* at Saint *Omers* and other Popish places: which private prayers are (as it semes) taken out of *Iohn Cozens* his *Cozening Devotions* (as they are rightly discovered to be by Orthodox men) and extracted out of divers Popish *Prayer-Bookes*.[53]

The writer of *The Arminian Nunnery* was not alone in suspecting the Ferrars of religious double-dealing. Indeed, according to Barnabas Oley, in 1637 when Nicholas was on his deathbed and requested that a "great company of Comedies, Tragedies, Love Hymns, Herociall poems" and other worldly writings in his possession be burned, rumors circulated among the neighbors that he had been a conjuror and that his books of magic were what had been given to the flames.[54] It is also alleged that a detachment of Puritan soldiery ransacked Little Gidding, destroyed the chapel, smashed the organ, and burned all the papers they could find (though some suggest no ransacking ever occurred).[55] Nevertheless, the family clearly felt threatened and most of the community, witnessing the ways in

52. Ibid., 3.
53. Ibid., 9–10. John Cosin (1595–1672) was a bishop of the established church also often accused of popish sympathies.
54. [Barnabas Oley], "A Prefatory View of the Life of Mr. Geo. Herbert, &c" in G.H. [George Herbert], *A Priest to the Temple, or The Country Parson His Character and Rule of Holy Life* (London, 1652), B12.
55. A.L. Maycock, *Nicholas Ferrar of Little Gidding*, 140. David Ransome, for one, has discounted the alleged ransacking, writing, "The family itself returned to the manor in late 1645 or early 1646 and no surviving estate documents or letters refer to destruction or the need for repairs. There was an attempt at sequestration but John visited London in the winter of 1647–48 and secured its removal." See "Alleged Ransacking—an update," *Little Gidding Church*, http://www.littlegidding-church.org.uk/lgchtmlfiles/detailfiles/lgcpopuptextpage1.html (accessed 30 March 2015).

which both the Civil War and English culture were developing, had removed to the Netherlands in 1643 to wait out the storm. They returned in 1645.

In his study of the Little Gidding community, A.L. Maycock makes much of Nicholas's defense that his nieces "had made no *Vowes,*" as if this closed the case on allegations of the crypto-Catholicism. And though Maycock admits that "Mary and Anna Collett regarded themselves as irrevocably pledged to the single life," he cautions that "the question at issue is whether their vows were ever ratified and consecrated by the authority of the Church."[56] But that is not the issue. Indeed, Beguine communities of the late Middle Ages were likewise comprised of lay membership and were also under no formal disciplinary obligations such as vows—but they certainly considered themselves as belonging to the Catholic Church. The issue, certainly for their Puritan critics, was how much of the Ferrars' discipline was emblematic of Catholicism, (as, indeed, the community later became emblematic of what would be called "Anglo-Catholicism"). During the seventeenth century, a large measure of that emblematicization was traced to Mary and Anna Collett.

In addition to their dedication to lives of prayer, fasting, and perpetual virginity, Mary and Anna Collett, as well as their younger sister Susanna, also observed what Maycock calls, "a uniform habit of black."[57] Lenton describes the community's manner of dress in his original letter to Hetley:

> The daughter's four sons kneeled all the while on the edge of the half-pace; all in black gowns. (And they went to church in round Monmouth caps, as my man said; for I looked not back) the rest all in black, save one of the daughter's daughters, who was in a fryer's grey gown.[58]

56. Ibid., 180.
57. Ibid., 179.
58. Christopher Wordsworth, *Ecclesiastical Biography; or Lives of Eminent Men connected with the History of Religion in England; from the Commencement of the Reformation to the Revolution,* 6 vols. (London: F.C. and J. Rivington, 1810), 5: 257. The letter is reproduced in full, 250–61.

When their grandmother, Mary Woodnoth Ferrar, retired from her duties in the leadership in the community, Mary Collett assumed them and also assumed the "friar's grey gown" signifying her authority. When the younger Mary took upon herself the proper garb of authority, she also took upon herself the title of "Mother," a name many scholars of Richard Crashaw have read as psychologically significant in their examinations of that poet and his relationship with her.[59] But there is an even more subtle reason some extreme Puritans associated the women of Little Gidding with Catholicism.

As Frances Dolan has observed, the association of Catholicism and femininity in post-Reformation England was "tenacious."[60] Indeed, such attributions persisted well into the modern period and aspersions of "effeminacy" were also hurled at the Oxford Movement, its care for ritual and aesthetics allegedly lures for "leading captive silly women."[61] Furthermore, the anti-Catholic discourses of the early modern period also associated Catholicism with female empowerment—a real scandal—and a goodly amount of Protestant polemic (such as Spenser's representation of the Catholic Church as the villainous character Duessa in *The Faerie Queen*) even represented the pope as female.[62] Such an anxiety clearly inhabits *The Arminian Nunnery*—the use of the term "nunnery" certainly indicates this—and it is small wonder that the community was suspected of papistical inclinations, considering the religio-political milieu of the time.

59. Crashaw's only extant work of prose in his own hand is a letter he wrote from exile in Leyden lamenting the Ferrar family's obstruction of his access to Mary Collett while the family waited out the war in the Low Countries. Scholars have speculated it may have had something to do with his turn toward formal entrance into the Roman Catholic Church. The entire letter is reproduced in L. C. Martin's edition of Crashaw, *The Poems, English, Latin and Greek of Richard Crashaw*, 2nd ed. (Oxford: The Clarendon Press, 1957), xxv–xxxi.

60. Frances Dolan, *Whores of Babylon: Catholicism, Gender, and Seventeenth-Century Print Culture* (Ithaca and London: Cornell University Press, 1999), 10.

61. Quoted in John Shelton Reed, "'A Female Movement': The Feminization of Nineteenth-Century Anglo-Catholicism," *Anglican and Episcopal History* 57, no. 2 (June 1988): 199–238, at 208.

62. Frances Dolan, *Whores of Babylon*, 45 and 53.

The community at Little Gidding, of course, denied they were closeted Catholics. According to Lenton (and repeated in *The Arminian Nunnery*), Nicholas, when charged with popery, "answered with a ferocious protestation (though not so properly) that he did as verily beleeve the Pope to be *Antichrist*, as any Article of his Faith."[63] Oley corroborates the sentiment expressed here, writing that Nicholas was "torn asunder as with mad horses, or crushed betwixt the upper and under milstone of contrary reports; that he was a Papist, and that he was a Puritan."[64] It could be argued that the Little Gidding project was iconographic of the Anglican *via media*, but it seems to me it is more representative of a desire to preserve an aspect of English religious life that was all but vanished, and to do so in a way that might still be considered part of the Reform. The Anglican *via media*, in fact, was less a middle way between Catholicism and Calvinism than a middle way between Catholicism and secularism, a project in our own time lamentably unfolding as we see the continuing absorption of the British Church by secularism and as postmodern Anglicanism looks more and more like its parody in Aldous Huxley's *Brave New World*.

Nevertheless, as many Crashaw scholars and biographers have observed, the Little Gidding community did serve for Crashaw at least as a kind of half-way house between Canterbury and Rome, a place where

> The self-remembring SOVL sweetly recouers
> Her kindred with the starrs; not basely houers
> Below: But meditates her immortall way
> Home to the originall sourse of LIGHT & intellectuall Day.[65]

In a similar fashion, it could be argued, Mary Collett served as the poet's conduit to Teresa of Avila and devotion to the Virgin Mary, a devotion fully realized when he "died of a Feaver, the holy order of his soul over-heating his body, Canon of *Loretto*, whence he was

---

63. *The Arminian Nunnery*, 2–3.
64. [Barnabas Oley], "A Prefatory View of the Life of Mr. Geo. Herbert," A12.
65. Richard Crashaw, "Description of a Religious House and Condition of Life (Out of Barclay)," from *The Poems, English, Latin and Greek of Richard Crashaw*, lines 36–39.

carried to heaven, as that Church was brought thither by Angels, singing."[66]

My claim is that while the Little Gidding community was very clearly—at least in their own minds—firmly settled in a self-recognition and self-designation as Protestants, they, at the same time, give clear evidence of a Catholic palimpsest, for all their differences from what we see in Herrick, in a strange resonance with that merry poet's retro-Catholic sensibilities. But it was a Catholicism tragically and irrevocably broken: two pieces of a whole simultaneously unable to survive in isolation from one another and unable to be rejoined, their reciprocal integrity never to be restored.

The Ferrars and Herrick, that is, emblematize two aspects of England's Catholic past while still imposing on it (more so in the case of the Ferrars) some semblance of Protestant respectability. What bleeds through the Ferrars is England's monasticism: the *regula* of ordered prayer and service and a life completely devoted to cultivating the mindfulness of the presence of God. What shines through Herrick, on the other hand, is England's Catholic pastoral and folk religion, an order not devoted to a structured religious life, but the messier, more rambunctious, altogether chaotic celebration of living and dying and of the sacredness found in fecundity, carnival, funeral, and their embeddedness in each other. The architects of the Reformation tried to collapse these orders into one by banishing both monasticism and carnival, or at the very least seriously curtailing them, into what Taylor has called a "one-speed religion" in search of an unrealizable "single, omnicompetent code."[67] The

---

66. David Lloyd, *Memories of the Lives, Actions, Sufferings & Deaths of Those Noble, Reverend, and Excellent Personages that Suffered by Death, Sequestration, Decimation, or Otherwise for the Protestant Religion...* (London, 1668), 619. A number of contemporary scholars have made rather a cottage industry of reading Crashaw as a repressed Freudian Oedipus unconsciously desiring to kill his dead Puritan father by converting to Catholicism and just as unconsciously desiring to marry his deceased mother (in his relationship with Mary Collett and in his devotional poems to Mary Magdalen, Teresa of Avila, and the Virgin Mary), a resilient critical gesture that does much to prove the claim that the English department is where discredited theories from other disciplines go to die.

67. Charles Taylor, *A Secular Age*, 61–84 and 52.

Ferrars and Herrick, in their own very different manners, resisted this movement. Yet they maintained at least one thing in common: the centrality of *communitas* to a life in religion. That they both failed was not due to their own faults, but was the product of the energies of secularism unwittingly released by the desire to first reform, and then reform the reform, in a never-ending cycle of communal destruction.

The Poetic of Sophia

IN HIS seminal essay, "The Work of Art in the Age of Mechanical Reproduction" (1936), Walter Benjamin considers the changes—both subtle and abrupt—that accompanied the technological age and its colonization of the representative arts. He observes that such reproductive technologies not only widely disseminate works of art (or, rather, facsimiles of works of art), a gesture of democratization bringing artworks to the masses (the proletariat), but that they also turn works of art into objects of distraction at the expense of their role as objects of concentration and contemplation, a cultural development that, he believed, can lead to Fascism.[1] His intuition is keen, and one can only wonder what Benjamin would say were he to witness the eschatological aesthetic ramifications brought on by the democratizing reproductive technology we know as the internet.

Tellingly, Benjamin has almost nothing to say about poetry.

It is my position that poetry, the utterance of the poetic, is impervious to technological colonization. This is not to say that the technological has not impacted the craft of writing. Clearly, it has. Benjamin points to this aberration as arising out of Mallarme and Dada (to which I would add Gertrude Stein) and, indeed, this "aesthetic" carries on today in the profligate graduate MFA programs that have turned the writing of verses into a kind of careerism, negating poetry's and the poet's true vocation: the affirmative response to a summons, a calling analogous to the priesthood. The academy has been colonized by the technological. This technologization, this standardization of production, manifests in academia in the fetishization (read: idolatry) of what is called "professionalism" aligned according to the bureaucratic dictates of "best practices." Whatever those are. At the very least the technological colonization

---

1. Walter Benjamin, *Illuminations: Essays and Reflections*, ed. Hannah Arendt and trans. Harry Zohn (New York: Schocken Books, 1968), 241.

is dehumanizing; at worst it is something far more sinister. As Nikolai Berdyaev argued in 1935, "The world threatens to become an organized and technicized chaos in which only the most terrible forms of idolatry and demon-worship can live."[2] That day is here.

Yet, I still hold that poetry—authentic poetry—is impervious to this colonization. The poem—unlike the film, the photograph, the digital or lithographed image, the sound recording—does not exist in its medium of presentation. It exists beyond its medium, whether paper and ink or pixel. Its medium is not its medium, but only its point of appearance: as light only appears in its showing of the things of this world. Furthermore, the poem only truly comes alive through acts of contemplation. (There is much of what Michel Henry calls "Life" or "coming into the world" in this.)[3] One does not simply read a poem; one enters it. And, in a mysteriously reciprocal gesture, the poem enters into the reader, evidence of the "installation of a new ontological dimension."[4]

This opening certainly is potential in all art forms; but only in poetry is the medium ancillary to such a diminished degree. The forms of some poems—in George Herbert and e.e. cummings, for example—of course, are integral to their utterance: but they are not equal to it and the poems, in any case, are not compromised by the mode of presentation. Poetry, though not as tied into the media of presentation as other art forms, still requires language which, in the case of written poetry, generally means typography. The physicality of drama, painting, music, sculpture, and so forth are essential for the presence of their utterance to be experienced—a digital experience of these art forms, like the photographs of someone's vacation,

2. Nicolas Berdyaev, *The Fate of Man in the Modern World*, trans. Donald A. Lowrie (1935; reprt., Ann Arbor, MI: The University of Michigan Press, 1961), 127.

3. Michel Henry, *I Am the Truth: Toward a Philosophy of Christianity*, trans. Susan Emanuel, Cultural Memory in the Present (Stanford: Stanford University Press, 2003).

4. Michel Henry, interviewed by Jean-Marie Brohm and Magali Uhl, "Art et phénoménologie de la vie (entretien, Montpellier, 1996)" in *Auto-donation: Entretiens et Conferences* by Michael Henry (Paris: Editions Beauchesne, 2004), 197–222, at 197.

are diminishment, compromise, *signum*. The poem is not compromised by the presentation of the medium. Its being exists elsewhere.

My considerations here, however, should not be construed as aesthetics, though I am concerned with the arrival of the Beautiful. Aesthetics is, ultimately, rationalization, Aristotelian, a categorical wrestling with the uncategorical. It is concerned with appearances and not with the appearing as such. The Beautiful, on the other hand, is what appears. Its appearing, furthermore, is experienced as personal, as an encounter. An encounter, it must be admitted, with being. With a being.

The arrival of the Beautiful is facilitated by—indeed, unimaginable apart from—a contemplative presence to phenomena. Reverie, the playful abiding in an imaginal realm between the noumenal and physical worlds, provides an opening to this presence. Reverie, in the disappearance of time that seems to take place within its dimensions, allows us to be present to the things of this world and additionally, as Gaston Bachelard has observed, "puts us in the state of a soul being born."[5] For Percy Bysshe Shelley, reverie was essential to the poetic act and rendered the soul more porous to the cosmos:

> There are some persons who in this respect are always children. Those who are subject to the state called reverie, feel as if their nature were dissolved into the surrounding universe, or as if the surrounding universe were absorbed into their being. They are conscious of no distinction. And these are states which precede, or accompany, or follow an unusually intense and vivid apprehension of life.[6]

Poetry, the poetic, indeed, any art "as the letting happen of the advent of the truth,"[7] can allow such an opening, but not without the proper disposition of soul, the appropriate pentecostal open-

---

5. Gaston Bachelard, *The Poetics of Reverie: Childhood, Language, and the Cosmos*, trans. David Russell (1969; reprt., Boston: Beacon Press, 1971), 15.

6. Percy Bysshe Shelley, *Shelley's Poetry and Prose*, ed. Neil Fraistat and Donald H. Reiman, Norton Critical Editions (New York: W. W. Norton and Company, 1977), 477.

7. Martin Heidegger, "The Origin of the Work of Art" in *Poetry, Language, Thought*, trans. Albert Hofstadter (New York: Harper & Row Publishers, 1971), 72.

ness. And written poetry, perhaps more than any other art form, is especially conducive to entering such a state. For poetry cannot be experienced passively, as is often the case with music or drama, sculpture or painting. To read attentively, the only way poetry can be read, is to have a text enter the soul: it is a pure act, an act of absolute vulnerability. Literary theory, or at least the greater number of voices that have occupied this rhetorical space for most of the past forty years, can thus be seen to be a kind of anti-theory, anti-θεωρία, absolutely alien, as it is, from contemplation (θεωρία). It has poisoned the relationship of reader and text and tries to deliver poetry to the prisons of premediation.

My appeal, then, is to what I have called (inspired by William Desmond) an *agapeic criticism*. In agapeic criticism we approach the text in an attitude of respect and reverence, avoiding the temptation to colonize it with premediated assumptions. Taking this approach, we participate with the text in a spirit of charity. Through the risk inherent to this participation, we expose ourselves to possibility. On the one hand stands the possibility of contamination—pornographic or other works that render sin beautiful or appealing in some way certainly possess the ability to poison the soul. As Jacques Maritain has articulated so eloquently, "In making out of your sin beauty, you send it like an angel among your brothers. It kills them without a sound."[8] Such an opening is not an opening to life, but, rather, to death. On the other hand, participation can become an act, as Dionysius says, "by which it irrepressibly imparts being, life, wisdom and other gifts of *its* all creative goodness."[9] Some will call my appropriation of Dionysius here something of an ontological leap. It is not. My claim is that the life accessed through an agapeic engagement has as its source Dionysius's subject. *For what else is a revelation of the True, the Good, and the Beautiful?* This brings to the subject of Sophia.

---

8. Jacques Maritain, *Art and Poetry*, trans. Elva de P. Matthews (New York: Philosophical Library, 1943), 51.

9. From *The Divine Names* 644A. Taken from Pseudo-Dionysius, *The Complete Works*, trans. Colm Luibheid and Paul Rorem (New York: Paulist Press, 1987), 62. My emphasis.

Sophia, as described in scripture, is identical with the life embedded in creation:

> He that shall find me, shall find life, and shall have salvation from
> the Lord.
> But he that shall sin against me shall hurt his own soul. All that
> hate me love death. (Proverbs 8:35–36)

> For Wisdom is more active than all active things: and reacheth
> everywhere by reason of her purity.
> For she is a vapour of the power of God, and a certain pure ema-
> nation of the glory of the almighty God: and therefore no
> defiled thing cometh into her.
> For she is the brightness of eternal light, and the unspotted mirror
> of God's majesty, and the image of his goodness.
> And being but one, she can do all things: and remaining in herself
> the same, she reneweth all things, and through nations con-
> veyeth herself into holy souls, she maketh the friends of God
> and prophets. (Wisdom 7:23–26)

God's Wisdom, then, is *zoē* rather than *bios*, the light of the first day rather than that of the fourth.

Coinciding with these cosmological dimensions of Sophia are the sophiological implications implicit in the creative act itself, not only in that of God, but also in that of the human person who thereby becomes a truly sophianic subject. The creative act is essentially a transfigurative act, whereby the human person participates in what Proverbs describes as Sophia's playfulness: "I was with him forming all things: and was delighted every day, playing before him at all times; Playing in the world: and my delights were to be with the children of men" (8:30–31). As Pavel Florensky writes, "Sophia, the true Creation or creation in the Truth, is a preliminary hint at the transfigured, spiritualized world as the manifestation, impercepti-ble for others, of the heavenly in the earthly."[10] This transfiguration is precisely what William Blake intuited when he wrote of "Wisdom in the Human Imagination / Which is the Divine Body of the Lord

---

10. Pavel Florensky, *The Pillar and Ground of Truth: An Essay in Orthodox Theodicy in Twelve Letters* (Princeton: Princeton University Press, 1997), 283.

Jesus. blessed for ever."[11] It likewise underscores Nikolai Berdyaev's thesis in *The Meaning of the Creative Act* that through human creativity "man can discover limitless aid immanent within himself, by the creative act, all the power of God and the world, the true world, freed from the illusory world."[12] This is what Henry Vaughan and Thomas Traherne were consciously trying to effect. And William Wordsworth without really trusting in it. Every imaginal act, however, is not redemptive; nor is every creative act identical with that which Berdyaev has in mind. And every piece of writing called a "poem" does not automatically qualify as poetry.

Poetry grounded in an exploration of being, then, would naturally tend to be more likely to disclose being—would it not?—in a way through which the sophianic nature of not only the poem but of the creative act itself might become actualized. This happens, for instance, in religious poetry that has the encounter with God—the source of all being—as object or addressee, a phenomenon traceable in the Metaphysical poets, for example, in the Sufi poet Rumi, and more recently in David Jones, Czeslaw Milosz, and Franz Wright. Such poems are essentially forms of *adoration*. Adoration, as Jean-Luc Nancy claims, "opens to the infinite, without which there would be no *relation* in the full sense that this word alone, perhaps, can take on, but only rapport, liaison, connection."[13] *Adoration*, that is, *awakens relation*. In this way, I would add, poems that are not necessarily concerned with God directly can also disclose being through their own particular acts of adoration, say, in nature poetry or in love poetry. In this way, the poetic clearly has a relationship to prayer. The sophianic poetic act, then, functions as an awakening: the reader's intentionality awakens the adoration in the poem, which reciprocally awakens devotion in the reader. This

11. William Blake, *Milton: a Poem in 2 Books*, 3.3, in *The Complete Poetry and Prose of William Blake*, ed. David V. Erdman with commentary by Harold Bloom, revised edition (Berkeley and Los Angeles: University of California Press, 1982).

12. Nicolas Berdyaev, *The Meaning of the Creative Act*, trans. Donald A. Lowrie (New York: Collier Books, 1962), 14.

13. Jean-Luc Nancy, *Adoration: The Deconstruction of Christianity II*, trans. John McKeane, Perspectives in Continental Philosophy (New York: Fordham University Press, 2013), 73.

adoration blossoms forth into acts of communion: of the reader with the poetic genius; the reader and the poet with divinity. The reader's presence to the poem meets the poet's presence, informed by the presence beyond presences. The entire movement is thoroughly sacramental.

Some poetry, furthermore, is more explicitly sophiological, not only in its adorative aspects, but also in the ways it takes up some of the themes of sophiology proper (whether deliberately or not on the part of the poet is not important) which allows access to alternate dimensions and unfoldings of the poetic event. The apprehension of this event is characterized by a transfigurative attentiveness to Things, an awareness of what Hans Urs von Balthasar calls the "splendor" that shines *through* (and not from) them. There are several streams of this kind of poetry.

In one expression of this phenomenon, the writer, rather than adopting prose, couches his own religious experiences of a Sophia figure in poetic utterances, choosing a language of intimacy and reverie instead of one of empiricism, defenses, and proofs. Another is distinctly Marian in its theological aesthetic, attentive to the incarnational and sacramental role of the Virgin Mary in uniting divinity to the flesh and to the world, a reciprocating gesture both sacrificial and salvific. Still another turns its concern to that which shines through nature, through art, through human relationship, and through liturgy, revealing the Wisdom of God latent in the things of this world. And much sophiological poetry traverses all of these domains simultaneously.

First of all, the sophiological poetry explicitly concerned with Sophia as divine person begins with Russian Orthodox philosopher, literary critic, and poet, Vladimir Solovyov. Solovyov had at least three religious experiences regarding Sophia (whom he only ever referred to as "My Eternal Friend"). The first occurred during Divine Liturgy on the Feast of the Ascension, May 1862, when the philosopher was nine years old.[14] He met Sophia again while

---

14. The story of Solovyov's visions of his Eternal Friend is oft repeated. See his nephew, Fr. Sergey M. Solovyov's account, *Vladimir Solovyov: His Life and Creative*

researching her at the British Library. There she told him, "Meet me in the desert!" He immediately booked passage to Cairo, where she appeared to him once more—after he had been jumped and robbed by Bedouins. Solovyov recounts the experiences in his poem "Three Meetings."

The poem is narrative in form, long and with many digressions in which the poet pokes fun at himself (he was known for his puckish sense of humor and his outrageous laugh). He first touches on his religious experience as a nine-year-old:

> The sanctuary was open... But where were priest and deacon?
> Where was the crowd of praying people? Suddenly,
> The stream of passions dried up without a trace.
> Azure was all around; azure was in my soul.
>
> Suffused with a golden azure, and your hand
> Holding a flower that came from other lands,
> You stood there smiling a smile of radiance.
> You nodded to me, and vanished in the mist. (lines 25–32)[15]

Later in the poem, he describes his experience as a young scholar at the British Museum:

> But once—it was in autumn—I said to her:
> "O blossoming of divinity! I feel
> Your presence here. But why have you not revealed
> Yourself to my eyes since I was a child?"
>
> Hardly had I thought these words
> When all around was filled with golden azure
> And before me she was shining again—
> But only her face, it was her face alone.

Evolution, trans. Aleksey Gibson (Fairfax, VA: Eastern Christian Publications, 2000), 35–6 and 129–36; Paul M. Allen, *Vladimir Soloviev: Russian Mystic* (Blauvelt, NY: Steiner, 1978), 23–8 and 109–119.

15. All translations of Solovyov's poetry here are from Boris Jakim and Laury Magnus and taken from Jakim's *The Religious Poetry of Vladimir Solovyov* (Kettering, OH: Semantron Press, 2014). The poems are also reproduced in *The Heavenly Country: Primary Sources, Poetry, and Critical Essays on Sophiology,* ed. Michael Martin (Kettering, OH: Angelico Press/Sophia Perennis, 2016), 215–22.

That instant was one of happiness much prolonged.
My soul again became blind to things of earth.
And if I spoke, any "sober" ear
Would consider my speech incoherent and stupid. (lines 69–80)

And in the Egyptian desert, following his unfortunate encounter with the Bedouins, his third encounter arrives:

Long I lay there in a frightened slumber, till
At last, I heard a gentle whisper: "Sleep, my poor friend."
Then I fell into a deep sleep; and when I waked
The fragrance of roses wafted from earth and heaven.

And in the purple of the heavenly glow
You gazed with eyes full of an azure fire.
And your gaze was like the first shining
Of universal and creative day.

What is, what was, and what will be were here
Embraced within that one fixed gaze… The seas
And rivers all turned blue beneath me, as did
The distant forest and the snow-capped mountain heights.

I saw it all, and all of it was one,
One image there of beauty feminine…
The immeasurable was confined within that image.
Before me, in me, you alone were there. (lines 145–64)

Unlike almost all other sophiological poetry, Solovyov's is absent a relationship with the natural world. Things of nature—flowers, seas, mountains—though mentioned, have no actuality in this poetry. They are simply ciphers for another reality. His poetic landscape is utterly and absolutely a realm between heaven and earth, at the horizon of Sophia's appearing. He simply has no interest in anything else.

Solovyov's follower, the poet Alexander Blok, is a little more incarnated than his master, a little more attentive to the natural world—though not by much. Sophia, for Blok, still inhabits the *metaxu* between the ideal and the real, and, like Solovyov, the idiom of dream seems to best fit his rhetorical needs:

I seek strange and new things on the pages
Of old and familiar books;

I dream of white vanished birds
And sense the isolated instant.
Agitated rudely by the commotion of life
And dismayed by whispers and shouts,
I am anchored securely by my white dream
To the shore of the recent past.
White You are, imperturbable in the depths,
Stern and wrathful in life,
Mysteriously anxious and mysteriously loved,
Maiden, Dawn, Burning Bush.
The cheeks of golden-haired maidens fade,
Dawns are not as eternal as dreams.
Thorns crown the humble and wise
With the white fire of the Burning Bush.[16]

Blok's Sophia is clearly divine, and, as "the white fire of the Burning Bush," certainly facilitates God's appearing (as the Virgin does for Christ). But her presence in the material world is tenuous, not a quality of its being, not a catalyst for the appearance of *zoē* in Things.

Beginning at least with the mystical speculation of Jacob Boehme, the sophianic role of the Virgin Mary has been an important aspect of sophiological metaphysics and this has been reflected, perhaps most clearly of all, in poetry. Though, as not every sophiological poem is Marian, neither is every Marian poem sophiological. To be sophiological, the poem should reveal the implicate order (to appropriate David Bohm's term) of Mary in her simultaneously cosmological, teleological, and incarnational offices as they are married to the disclosure of Truth, Beauty, and Goodness. A number of important poems engage this metaphysical space.

Perhaps the first poem to deliberately enter this theological aesthetic is Henry Vaughan's poem, "The Knot." The poem was first published in the second part of Vaughan's *Silex Scintillans* (1655), issued five years after the work's first installment and apparently after Vaughan had encountered the writing of Boehme, which first

---

16. Poem 111 of *Verses about the Beautiful Lady*. Taken from Alexander Blok, *Poems of Sophia*, trans. and ed. Boris Jakim (Kettering, OH: Semantron Press, 2014). See also *The Heavenly Country*, 242.

began to appear in English translation in the late 1640s.[17] The poem illustrates the reciprocity between the heavenly and earthly realms effected by the Virgin Mary's affirmative participation in the Incarnation:

The Knot

> Bright Queen of Heaven! Gods Virgin Spouse!
>   The glad worlds blessed maid!
> Whose beauty tyed life to thy house,
>   And brought us saving ayd.
>
> Thou art the true Loves-knot; by thee
>   God is made our Allie,
> And mans inferior Essence he
>   With his did dignifie.
>
> For Coalescent by that Band
>   We are his body grown,
> Nourished with favors from his hand
>   Whom for our head we own.
>
> And such a Knot, what arm dares loose,
>   What life, what death can sever?
> Which us in him, and him in us
>   United keeps for ever.

Like Vaughan, Thomas Traherne perceives this quality behind the qualities of Things and names its author:

> O what a world art Thou! A world within!
>   All things appear
>   All objects are
> Alive in Thee! Supersubstantial, rare,
>   Above themselves, and nigh of kin
>   To those pure things we find
>   In His great mind
> Who made the world! ("My Spirit," lines 110–17)

---

17. I discuss Boehme's influence on both Henry and Thomas Vaughan in the chapter entitled "The Rosicrucian Mysticism of Henry and Thomas Vaughan" in my *Literature and the Encounter with God in Post-Reformation England* (Farnham, UK: Ashgate Publishing, 2014), especially pages 143–46.

Traherne is acutely aware of the presence behind appearing, of the Life that informs life.

The end of Goethe's *Faust, Part II* and Novalis's exquisite *Hymnen an die Nacht* (*Hymns to the Night*) likewise espouse a sophiology more heavenly than earthly, though both are supremely concerned with Sophia-Mary's role as rescuer of souls as well as her ontological dimension as a quality of the cosmos. As Novalis writes,

> Praise the world queen, the higher messenger of a holy word, a nurse of blessed love—she sends me you—tender, loved—Night's lovely sun,—now I wake—for I'm yours and mine—you called the Night to life for me,—humanized me—tear my body with spirit fire, so I can mix with you more inwardly, airily, and then the wedding night will last forever. (*Hymns to the Night*)[18]

What Vaughan and Traherne, Goethe and Novalis do not do in these poems—but what Vaughan does in many others (and Goethe certainly does in his scientific work)—is show the relationship between this binding of the natural and the supernatural in the language of Things, of the world of growth, of the world of *bios* imbued by the world of *zoē*. This is the world explored in its Marian connotations in some of Gerard Manley Hopkins's poetry and in some important mid-twentieth-century Catholic poets.

Hopkins provided Catholic poets with a sophiological poetic idiom even though he could not have been aware of what subsequent generations came to know as sophiology. Hopkins's attention to "the dearest freshness deep down things" ("God's Grandeur," line 10) certainly speaks to such a sophiological sensibility, but nowhere is his sophiology as explicit as in his poem "The Blessed Virgin compared to the Air we Breathe." Its sophiology is apparent from the poem's first lines:

> Wild air, world-mothering air,
> Nestling me everywhere,
> That each eyelash or hair
> Girdles; goes home betwixt

---

18. Novalis, *Hymns to the Night*, trans. Dick Higgins, revised ed. (New York: McPherson & Company, 1984), 13. See also *The Heavenly Country*, 208.

> The fleeciest, frailest-flixed
> Snowflake; that's fairly mixed
> With, riddles, and is rife
> In every least thing's life. (lines 1–8)

The Virgin is, indeed, "rife / In every least thing's life," as Boehme would doubtlessly concur. As in Boehme, in Hopkins the Virgin is the catalyst, the vessel through which grace pours into the world, a divine principle of the world:

> Let all God's glory through,
> God's glory which would go
> Through her and from her flow
> Off, and no way but so. (lines 30–33)

This is all so because "her hand leaves his light / Sifted to suit our sight" (112–13). The Virgin makes grace perceivable, and, quite literally, makes Christ experienceable through the senses. Hopkins's theological aesthetic here is also articulated by Pierre Teilhard de Chardin in his imaginative work (I am inclined to call it a prose poem) "*L'Eternel féminin*" ("The Eternal Feminine") as well as in Thomas Merton's prose poem, "Hagia Sophia."

Teilhard, who has received, I think, an undue amount of scorn from Catholic quarters (the Eastern Orthodox, ironically, seem to have a deeper appreciation for the much-maligned Jesuit), speaks a language highly conducive to sophiological insight. A scientist as well as a mystic, his genius proves particularly apt for describing the sophiological nature of Things and the sophiological office of the Virgin Mary:

> Lying between God and the earth, as a zone of mutual attraction,
> I draw them both together in a passionate union.
> —until the meeting takes place in me, in which the generation
> and plenitude of Christ are consummated throughout the centuries.
> I am the Church, the bride of Christ.
> I am Mary the Virgin, mother of all human kind.[19]

---

19. Pierre Teilhard de Chardin, *Writings in Time of War*, trans. René Hague (New York: Harper & Row, Publishers, 1968), 200–01. See also *The Heavenly Country*, 164.

It is unclear whether or not Teilhard was familiar with Boehme or Russian sophiology, though it is certainly possible that he was. Merton, on the other hand, was well-read in Russian sophiology, the influence of which is palpable in "Hagia Sophia."

Merton presciently and beautifully arranges the poem according to the times of prayer in monastic life (Lauds, Prime, Tierce, and so on). In the Compline section, Merton writes of the Virgin in sophianic terms, of Sophia in Marian terms:

Now the Blessed Virgin Mary is the one created being who enacts and shows forth in her life all that is hidden in Sophia. Because of this she can be said to be a personal manifestation of Sophia, Who in God is *Ousia* rather than Person. *Natura* in Mary becomes pure Mother. In her, *Natura* is as she was from the origin from her divine birth. In Mary *Natura* is all wise and is manifested as an all-prudent, all-loving, all-pure person: not a Creator, and not a Redeemer, but perfect Creature, perfectly Redeemed, the fruit of all God's great power, the perfect expression of wisdom in mercy. It is she, it is Mary, Sophia, who in sadness and joy, with the full awareness of what she is doing, sets upon the Second Person, the Logos, crown which is His Human Nature. Thus her consent opens the door of created nature, of time, of history, to the Word of God. God enters into His creation. Through her wise answer, through her obedient understanding, through the sweet yielding consent of Sophia, God enters without publicity into the city of rapacious men. She crowns Him not with what is glorious, but with what is greater than glory: the one thing greater than glory is weakness, nothingness, poverty. She sends the infinitely Rich and Powerful One forth as poor and helpless, in His mission of inexpressible mercy, to die for us on the Cross. The shadows fall. The stars appear. The birds begin to sleep. Night embraces the silent half of the earth. A vagrant, a destitute wanderer with dusty feet, finds his way down a new road. A homeless God, lost in the night, without papers, without identification, without even a number, a frail expendable exile lies down in desolation under the sweet stars of the world and entrusts Himself to sleep.[20]

20. From Thomas Merton, *The Collected Poems of Thomas Merton* (New York: New Directions, 1963). See also *the Heavenly Country*, 262.

Merton describes here the *metaxu* of Sophia, the inhabiting of a realm between realms, the bestowal of *zoē* in the kingdom of *bios*, the immanent appearing of transcendent grace.

A poet too little read these days, William Everson (Brother Antoninus) also touches on a sophiological aesthetics in his poem "A Canticle to the Great Mother of God," and in the *metaxu* of his dream-language explores the ontological mystery of the Virgin Mary joined to the Virgin Sophia. In doing so, he alludes to the great Eastern Orthodox church, Hagia Sophia, and the poem takes on the virtue of a prayer:

> Hidden within the furlongs of those deeps, your fiery virtue
> impregnates the sky, irradiant with wisdom.
> You are Byzantium, domed awesomeness, the golden-ruddy rich-
> ness of rare climes, great masterwork of God.
> Kneeling within thy moskey naves, seized in the luminous indult
> of those dusks,
> We hold the modal increase, subsumed in chant, ransomed of the
> balsam and the myrrh.
> Keeping an immost essence, an invitational letting that never
> wholly spends, but solemnly recedes,
> You pause, you hover, virtue indemnable, at last made still, a syn-
> thesis unprobed.
> Checked there, we tremble on the brink, we dream the venue of
> those everlapsing deeps.[21]

Everson, like Merton, attends to Sophia-Mary's role at the *metaxu* of nature and supernature and describes how the Church, likewise, participates in this holy effecting. That is, as Solovyov may have been the first to say, *Sophia is also an ontological dimension of the Church.*

Another twentieth-century poet with pronounced sophiological intuitions is David Jones, whose poem "The Tutelar of the Place" is a tour-de-force poem of sophianic power. But unlike the poems here noted by Merton and Everson, the Welshman Jones takes Sophia's

---

21. Brother Antoninus [William Everson], *The Hazards of Holiness: Poems, 1957–1960* (Garden City, NY: Doubleday, 1962), 59–63. See also *The Heavenly Country*, 255–56.

latency in the natural world as assumed and, instead, focuses upon that which obscures our perceptions of the sophianic shining: modernity and the Cartesian apotheosis of the technological. For Jones, each particular locale possesses its particular quality, what Hopkins celebrated as "thisness" and Duns Scotus called *haecceitas*, and Jones, like them, affirms that it participates in a transcendent source:

> Tell us of the myriad names answers to but one name: From this tump she answers Jac o' the Tump only if he call Great-Jill-of-the-tump-that-bare-me, not if he cry by some new fangle moder of far gentes over the flud, fer-goddess name from anaphora of far folk wont woo her; she's a rare one for locality.[22]

Folk customs, in Jones's poetic idiom, though absolutely particular to place, are nevertheless manifestations of eternal truth, authentic eruptions of joy in its beauty:

> Though she inclines with attention from far fair-height outside all boundaries, beyond the known and kindly nomenclatures, where all names are one name, where all stones of demarcation dance and interchange, troia[23] the skipping mountains, nod recognitions. As when on known-site ritual frolics keep bucolic interval at eves and divisions when they mark the inflexions of the year and conjugate with trope and turn the seasons' syntax, with beating feet, with wands and pentagons to spell out the Trisagion.

In his communitarian ethos, Jones stands in the poetic lineage of Robert Herrick, who also rejected the poisonous fruit of modernity and division and their combined destruction of the integral union of religion and the wheel of the year.

Like Heidegger, Steiner, Huxley, and so many others who have raised concerns about the human, cultural, and spiritual costs of our infatuation with technology, Jones argues that we have created this technology into an idol, a Moloch-like demon he calls the Ram, and that this god demands the instrumentalization and subsequent sacrifice of human persons:

---

22. See *The Heavenly Country*, 248–53.
23. "meander"

Remember the mound-kin, the kith of the *tarren*[24] gone from this mountain because of the exorbitance of the Ram . . . remember them in the rectangular tenements, in the houses of the engines that fabricate the ingenuities of the Ram...
Mother of Flowers save them then where no flower blows.
> Though they shall not come again because of the requirements of the Ram with respect to the world plan, remember them where the dead forms multiply, where no stamen leans, where the carried pollen falls to the adamant surfaces, where is no crevice.

Jones's incrimination here, I would argue, is a condemnation of the *anti-sophiology* that rules modernity, a modernity that can no longer recognize what a human person is, what gender is, what marriage is, or what is real. This is truly a modernity in which "dead forms multiply." And it is characterized by the fetishization of sterility.

As a final example of this kind of sophianic poem, I offer Franz Wright's beautiful poem "Rosary," a short, simple poem that quietly summarizes the sophiological qualities of the Virgin:

Rosary

Mother of space
inner

virgin
with no one face—

See them flying to see you
be near you

when you
are everywhere.[25]

It requires no commentary.

It is curious, I think, that these twentieth- and twenty-first-century Catholic poets write in a sophianic idiom so much more *incar-*

111

nated than even the Russians (even though Russian sophiology, particularly that of Bulgakov, is acutely aware of Sophia's shining through the natural world). There is in Catholicism something much more attentive to the sensual world, something seen perhaps only in Henry Vaughan (who is in many ways the most sophiological poet of all) among non-Catholics. Even Wendell Berry, known for his religious sensitivities and attentiveness to the natural world, is more a sabbatarian poet than a sophianic one. Protestantism's emphasis on God's transcendence at the expense of his immanence could have something to do with this. Similarly, these very different poetic ontologies may be tinged by one side's historical emphasis on preaching and the Word and the other's emphasis on the sensual and sacramental dimensions of the beholding, touching, and tasting implicit in participation in the Eucharist. The Orthodox poets partake of both of these sensibilities, of course, though the emphasis with them is on otherworldliness and *theosis* as the center of their theological aesthetic witness.

A great many poems, however, disclose a sophianic sensibility without committing to a particularly religious or ontological position. Some, such as Wordsworth's "Ode: Intimations of Immortality from Recollections of Early Childhood," Hölderlin's "*Da ich ein Knabe war...*" ("When I was a boy..."), and even Dylan Thomas's "Fern Hill," lament the loss of what Owen Barfield would call the "original participation"[26] characteristic of childhood, the innate human affirmation of presence shining through Things. I do wonder how much the Enlightenment and the philosophy of Immanuel Kant may have poisoned even these Romantics (and, yes, I am calling Dylan Thomas a Romantic). All three simultaneously evoke wonder and loss, holding to the bittersweet residue of splendor before finally bending, however begrudgingly and lamentably, to modernity's totalizing demand we that regard the material world as the only and final master, even though we sing in our chains like the sea buried in thoughts that do often lie too deep for tears.

---

26. See Barfield's *Saving the Appearances: A Study in Idolatry*, 2nd edition (Middletown, CT: Wesleyan University Press, 1988), 42.

Other poems distanced from religious orthodoxy do not seem to be characterized by the same existential fatalism. Percy Bysshe Shelley in his freer, less politically actuated moments certainly evinces something of this (for example, in "Ode to the West Wind") and certainly Keats expresses a similar confidence in the revelation of beauty. More recently, Robert Kelly, in his reminiscences of childhood reverie in the poem "The Heavenly Country," recognizes something shining through not only the landscape but also through literature—Tolkien and A.A. Milne no less than Blake and Wordsworth. The assurance, for Kelly, resides in the revelation of a nameless "It" seeking disclosure: "That it is a matter of It willing to reveal to Us I have never doubted."[27] The only difference is that I give It a name.

When I was a young graduate student, I found myself somewhat embarrassed by my devotion to Guillaume Apollinaire and his assertion that *"que seuls le renouvellent ceux qui sont fondés en poésie"*[28]—"only those remake the world who are rooted in poetry." Such a commitment did not seem becoming of a scholar in a postmodern milieu. When I confessed this to my professor, a gentle and learned Jesuit, all he could say was "Why not, Michael?" It took me most of twenty years to realize how right he was and that my initial intuition was, indeed, a realization of truth. Poetry as that which discloses the shining behind the universe, that itself participates in the shining, is what truly remakes the universe: for it participates, in however limited a way, in the source of that power. Thus, among other realms of human endeavor, the written word, scripture, the fine and performing arts, architecture, and liturgy all have the potential to participate in the poetic shining. Unfortunately, we live in times—like all times—in which those who think they can change the meanings of words can likewise change the universe. They are trapped in a prison of nominalism they mistake for freedom. And they are wrong. But as long as there is a shining, there will be the

27. Robert Kelly, *The Convections* (Santa Barbara, CA: Black Sparrow Press, 1978), 63. See also *The Heavenly Country*, 263–64.
28. "Poeme lu au Mariage d'André Salmon," line 10.

possibility of remaking the universe, "*parce que fondés en poésie nous avons des droits sur les paroles qui forment et défont l'Univers*"[29]— "because rooted in poetry, we have rights to make and unmake the universe." The name of this shining is Sophia.

29. Line 37.

On Poetry and Prophecy

EVEN more disappointing than the proliferation of MFA in creative writing programs, disembodied egregores that churn out variations on what Donald Hall has called the "McPoem," is the way these programs have turned the writing of poems into a professional career path, replete with networking, attendance at conferences, and the inflation of the CV. Those following this path are no different from the lawyers, physicians, computer programmers, lab technicians, and the professors who likewise have turned their interests into a way of making a living. These are all worthy aspirations, of course. But the poet's vocation, like the priest's, is not the same thing as a job or a livelihood. Indeed, the MFA's nearly absolute domestication of the poet may be the clearest sign of a culture in decline.

The incarnation of the poetic word is allegorical of the transubstantiative act in that it is implicitly sacramental. This idea, certainly, haunts Heidegger's meditations on poetry and shimmers behind all true poetry. As Guillaume Apollinaire once wrote,

> Those who essay the art of poetry search for and love that perfection which is God Himself. Would this divine goodness, this supreme perfection abandon those who devote their lives to revealing his glory? It seems impossible. To my mind, poets have the right to hope that when they die they will attain the enduring happiness that comes with the complete knowledge of God, that is, of sublime beauty.[1]

And there is a true poetry: a poetry that sings the invisible into being; a poetry impervious to the satanic poison of commodification. As there is also a true poet: a poet who, conscious of it or not, searches for the love and perfection that is God Himself, of sublime beauty.

1. Guillaume Apollinaire, *Bestiary, or The Parade of Orpheus*, trans. Pepe Karmel (1911; reprt. Boston: David R. Godine, 1980), 66.

Poetry is that which informs the sublimity potential in all the arts, but is sadly lacking in the art of the production line—and what is an MFA program but a production line for dilettantes? In an earlier age, true poets and thinkers of genius warned about the impending apocalypse of the poetic, the pillar and foundation of the arts, but they were dismissed. They are dismissed still. But their voices surround me:

> Poetry is the same essence of all the arts, regardless of their processes. Only literature, which is a superior form of the Word and the absolute aesthetic synthesis, can reach to the poetry of abstract ideas; but the lines of a monument, the colors of a picture, the forms of a statue, their language must give impressions, poetic emotions.
>
> Like the golden cherubim, the great artist does not speak, he sings; his compass, his pen, chisel, his brush, he seeks the ode, and when he attains it, he creates the lyric art, the first of the arts after the mystical art which is superhuman, since its objective is supernatural and divine.[2]

JOSÉPHIN PÉLADAN, 1883

I cannot get it out of my mind that this age of criticism is about to pass, and an age of imagination, of emotion, of moods, of revelation, about to come in its place; for certainly belief in a supersensual world is at hand again; and when the notion that we are "phantoms of the earth and water" has gone down the wind, we will trust our own being and all it desires to invent; and when the external world is no more the standard of reality, we will learn again that the great Passions are angels of God, and that to embody them "uncurbed in their eternal glory," even in their labour for the

---

2. "La poésie est l'essence même de tous les arts, quels que soient leurs procédés. Seule, la littérature, qui est la forme suprême du Verbe et la synthèse esthétique absolue, peut atteindre à la poésie d'idées abstraites; mais les lignes d'un monument, les couleurs d'un tableau, les formes d'une statue, doivent en leur langage donner des impressions, des émotions poétiques.

"Comme le chérubin doré, le grand artiste ne parle pas, il chante; de son compas, de sa plume, de son ébauchoir, de son pinceau, il cherche l'ode, et lorsqu'il l'atteint, il fait de l'art lyrique, le premier des arts après l'art mystique qui est surhumain, puisque son objectif est surnaturel, et divin." Joséphin Péladan, *La Decadence esthetique: L'art ochlocratique, salons de 1882 et 1883* (Paris: Camille Dalou, 1888), 66.

ending of man's peace and prosperity, is more than to comment, however wisely, upon the tendencies of our time, or to express the socialistic, or humanitarian, or other forces of our time, or even 'to sum up' our time, as the phrase is; for Art is a revelation, and not a criticism, and the life of the artist is in the old saying, "The wind bloweth where it listeth, and thou hearest the sound thereof, but canst not tell whence it cometh and whither it goeth; so is every one that is born of the spirit."[3]

WILLIAM BUTLER YEATS, 1895

The Spirit of Jesus is continual forgiveness of Sin: he who waits to be righteous before he enters into the Saviours kingdom, the Divine Body; will never enter there. I am perhaps the most sinful of men! I pretend not to holiness! yet I pretend to love, to see, to converse daily, as man with man, & the more to have an interest in the Friend of Sinners. Therefore [*Dear*] Reader, [*forgive*] what you do not approve, & [*love*] me for this energetic exertion of my talent.[4]

WILLIAM BLAKE, 1804

Our times do not associate poets with prophecy, with vision, or with mysticism. Instead, poets, if they are considered at all, are considered in the context of political or cultural movements, or as aloof and elitist poseurs living parasitically off of the academic class. They are not seen as agents of revelation, as those who open the doors by which the poetic word incarnates. Péladan called the poetic artist a priest, a king, and a magician. Names modernity despises. For Péladan the decrepitude of the age is due to the repercussions of three malign revolutions: the overthrow of theocracy by the Protestant Reformation; the overthrow of monarchy, subsequently replaced by Socialism; and the overthrow of an idealist aesthetic, replaced by the flat promises of realism.[5] He laments the rise of the secular state and the homogenization of culture. The poetic is nothing if not aristo-

---

3. William Butler Yeats, "The Body of the Father Christian Rosencrux" in *Ideas of Good and Evil*, 3rd ed. (London: A.H. Bullen, 1907), 310–11.

4. William Blake, *Jerusalem, The Emanation of The Giant Albion* (plate 3) in *The Complete Poetry and Prose of William Blake*, ed. David V. Erdman, commentary Harold Bloom, rev. ed. (Berkeley: University of California Press, 1982), 145.

5. Joséphin Péladan, *L'Art Idéaliste & Mystique: Doctrine de l'Ordre et du Salon Annuel des Rose+Croix*, 2nd ed. (Paris: Chamuel, 1894), 17–18, 25.

cratic. It is not democratic, not something created by committee or popular consent. Indeed, it is not created at all. Only awakened, enlivened. A poem is not a product.

Is it not the case that both religion and poetry, so colonized in these later years by the political, have forgotten their vocation? With this amnesia they have descended into irrelevance by assimilating the languages and gestures of secularism, of neoliberalism, of a flaccid socialism, and of a deadening realism. We can no longer recognize what Blake would describe as the emanation tearing itself away from the ideal reality; we have no organ sufficient to discern transcendence and its desire for immanence, and no longer bow before splendor as it comes into being.

What I am describing here, then, is no less than what Nikolai Berdyaev has called "the apocalypse of culture." Such is the product of our decent into spiritual torpor and thence into slavery: a slavery in our day of our wills to technology, our feeling to a shallow narcissism, and our thinking to the opinions of the electronic coterie which turns us all into mimetic sciolists. Cultural ennui is indistinguishable from spiritual and religious ennui. Culture without religion rapidly decays, while religion without culture loses its mooring in actual human life and has nothing to claim but the past:

> Behind the ideal values there stood prophets and geniuses in their day, with creative inspiration and fire. But when monuments have been erected to the prophets and the geniuses, and the streets have been called by their names, a chilled and mediocre culture comes into shape which no longer endures a prophetic spirit and a new spirit of genius.[6]

The apocalypse of culture ensues: "Culture must be transfigured into a new life, as the whole earth must be. It cannot linger on indefinitely in its mediocrity, in its cold legalism."[7]

The prophet is he who lives in the barren places, attentive to *parousia*, eating locusts and wild honey as he awaits the coming of the divine utterance. The poetic vocation also requires such wild-

---

6. Nikolai Berdyaev, *Slavery and Freedom*, trans. R.M. French (New York: Charles Scribner's Sons, 1944), 129.

7. Ibid.

ness, such authentic transgressivity. The much-lauded "transgressivity" of the academic poet has nothing transgressive about it. If the coterie holds the same opinions, there is no transgression. Transgression, to be authentic, requires the ground of the spirit, the source of all life. The transgression of the academy is mimetic transgression, anchored in the world, possessing no life. And, because of its privileged status, it spreads like a cancer.

Péladan knew well the poison offered by an academic aestheticism divorced from the nourishing sources of the spirit:

> Those who recognize the sacred mission of art must hate sacrilege and desecration, as a faithful Christian; and instead of this, the so-called aesthetes engage in incessant sacrilege and pride themselves on their desecrations.[8]

The programmatic and flaccid "transgression" that characterizes both the academy and postmodern art has succeeded in killing both the academy and art. It remains for the authentic transgressivity whose only source is the Holy Spirit to give life to a dead culture. But, like Peter's healing of Aeneas, the human person is necessary for him to act.

Some may point to my invocations of Péladan, Yeats, Blake, and Berdyaev as evidence of failure and the corruption of the very enterprise I propose. A *fin de siècle* Catholic eccentric and aesthete, a poet and occultist, an antinomian gnostic poet and artist, a Russian Orthodox existentialist rebel: fringe Christian figures, eccentrics, Romantics, and not one of them alive less than sixty-five years ago. But I call upon them as masters of both the poetic and the prophetic: they saw, if through a glass darkly, the impending apocalypse of culture, and each offered an antidote. Today we have no lack of barren places—but do we have prophecy or poetry? Some philosophers positioned in phenomenology seem to approach something near to, if not prophecy, then at least confession. But their language is troubled, obscurantist, clouded: as if clarity were

---

8. "Ceux qui reconnaissent la sainte mission de l'art doivent détester le sacrilège et la profanation, comme un fidèle chrétien; et, au lieu de cela, les prétendus esthètes se livrent à d'incessants sacrilèges et s'enorgueillissent de leurs profanations." Joséphin Péladan, *L'Art Idéaliste & Mystique*, 93.

something to avoid in fear of exposure before the ruling powers. Or perhaps they think ambiguity a quality of mystery. But this is an ancient Greek sensibility, not a Catholic one. The prophetic voice of poetry, however, is silent. When it does arise, as it did in the masters I invoke here, its utterance will be as obvious and as challenging as a drawn blade.

The primal quality of the prophetic voice is fearlessness. Fear of speaking permeates our society. Indeed, such fear has become its hallmark. It infests academe: show me a professor not afraid to speak truth before the archons of the academy and the assured punishment inflicted by the egregore, and I'll show you a career destroyed. Fear poisons workers in the arts, who then become its tools of power. It touches even the episcopacy. Fear, we know, is the primary tool of the Enemy.

> All the tortures of repentance are tortures of self-reproach on account of our leaving the Divine Harvest to the Enemy, the struggles of entanglement with incoherent roots. I know of no other Christianity and of no other Gospel than the liberty both of mind & body to exercise the Divine Arts of Imagination. (William Blake, *Jerusalem*, plate 77)

Like Blake, Péladan recognized the divine nature of the poetic vocation, a legacy fundamentally abandoned in our current cultural milieu, a milieu in which the guardians of art and poetry offer incense before the idols of utilitarianism, politics, and self-promotion and leave prophecy to the extravagances of a past that, in their postmodern positivism, they regard with condescension, themselves satisfied with the puny returns of publication, position, and notoriety.

Maritain was acutely aware of this crisis in his own times. He knew well the need for a prophetic renewal of the arts (for the poetic is the essence of all the arts) and the demonic nature of much of the creative work of his own times. "A good part of current literature," he wrote, "is positively possessed. In it could be verified some of the signs used by priests to detect possession: the horror of holy things, pseudo-prophecy, the use of unknown tongues, even levitation; it may be seen circulating upside down, along the vaults of thought."[9] Yet he refused to abandon art to the age; and in his quest for a religious art absolutely new he encouraged, among others, Jean Cocteau's brief—if nevertheless glorious—religious turn. How different from his Neo-Thomist inheritors, who seem to think that an authentically Catholic art must return to the forms of the past and summon the quattrocento from the dark abysm of time. And everything smells of dust. This will not do. As Eliot reminds us, "last year's words belong to last year's language / And next year's words await another voice."[10]

The motto of Péladan's *Salon de la Rose+Croix* was "*Ad Crucem Per Rosam*"—through the rose to the cross. He saw this as a supplement, a "joyful method of salvation . . . next to the path of tears" typically associated with *fin de siècle* French Catholic devotion.[11] The Rose—emblem of the Beautiful, the domain of art—draws the poet to the Cross.

For it is in the Cross that the poet participates in Redemption, and It becomes the cross by which he makes his own sacrifice. Though he arrives there by beauty, the end is the same. This is what makes all things new. Without it there is only death.

---

9. Jacques Maritain, *Art and Poetry*, trans. E. de P. Matthews (New York: Philosophical Library, 1943), 47.

10. T. S. Eliot, "Little Gidding," from *Four Quartets*. Lines 65–66.

11. "Une méthode joyeuse du salut et, a côté de la voie des larmes." Joséphin Péladan, *L'Art Idéaliste & Mystique*, 162.

Afterword

Michael Martin Addresses Fragmentation, Incarnation Spirituality, and Agapeic Intimacy

THE Roman Catholic Thomas Merton[1] and the Russian Orthodox Anthony Bloom[2] each spent the better part of their pastoral and writing vocations identifying the ways in which fragmentation separates us from God and separates us from ourselves and others. Each gave prescient witness to the growing compartmentalization that would become pandemic in the human soul by the turn of the century. *"Try to recover your fundamental unity,"* each of them cried out. *"Prayer is born of the discovery that the world has depths; that we are not only surrounded by invisible things but that we are also immersed in and penetrated by invisible things,"* says Metropolitan Anthony. Father Louis (Merton) is explicit: *"Try to recover your basic natural unity, to reintegrate your compartmentalized being into a coordinated and simple whole and learn to live as a unified human person. This means that you have to bring back together the fragments of your distracted existence so that when you say 'I,' there is really someone present to support the pronoun you have uttered."*

We live in an era of extraordinary energy, innovation and productivity. However, with increasing intensity, people, institutions and systems are afflicted by the pervasive and culturally re-enforced malaise which Merton and Bloom call *fragmentation*. The condition they describe means, among other things, that it has become nor-

---

1. Thomas Merton, *The Inner Experience: Notes on Contemplation*, edited with an introduction by William Shannon (San Francisco: HarperSanFrancisco, 2003).

2. Anthony Bloom (Metropolitan Anthony of Sourozh), *Living Prayer* (Springfield, IL: Templegate Publishers, 1966). See also his *Beginning to Pray* (New York/Mahwah, NJ: Paulist Press, 1970), and his *Courage to Pray* (Crestwood, NY: St. Vladimir Press, 1984).

mative to function in professional work and in private life through intentional compartmentalization strategies and unwitting forms of psychological avoidance. In addition, the intellectual materialism, the data-driven depersonalization within the scientific world view, and the various expressions of spin are just a few of the expressions of compartmentalization we meet daily.

From out of the scaffolding of human, institutional, ideological and systemic forms of fragmentation, there has emerged a voice that is a radically new and transformative bread. Michael Martin's *The Incarnation of the Poetic Word* isn't simply another demonstration project of the academic exercise in which professional expertise is displayed. He does not allow himself to *talk about* a post-modern problem or *talk about* a theory or *talk about* an elegant principle or an inspired doctrine. No, he is doing something new; he is differently engaged and the voice disclosed is that of a participant who is accessing being. The manner in which this author lives *inside and with the word* is not merely an orientation to the craft of writing. Because he is writing as a committed participant, a person grounded in committed relationship, he is intimately connected to the persons, ideas, beings, events, conditions and realities being called back into existence in the triple acts of agapeic writing, reading and perceiving. In his hand, in his pen, the vocation of writing has become theological, philosophical, Christological, sacramental, incarnational and Eucharistic. May I say more?

In his vocation as a writer, he inhabits a world, a world of committed and interconnected relationship. He also *inhabits his words*; he stands in them, not larger than life, but in proportion to that which is meaningful and integral. How and why can I say this? My sense of things is that precisely because of the quality and intensity of his capacity for intimacy, groundedness, accountability and coherence, something new and vital about a re-unified field is set free in his writing, and by extension, can be set afire in the souls of his readers. Not insignificantly, in this kind of milieu, we meet someone who is *serving* rather than *using*.

To return to the potentiating fecundity of our choices, Michael

Afterword

Martin's *Poetic Word* shows that when through committed relationship we allow ourselves *to serve* and *to be held accountable*, something about fragmentation and compartmentalization begins to be dissipated, and with the erosion of the interior wall, the malaise begins to be repaired, healed or transformed. (So too, our reluctance to be held accountable creates confusion or chaos. "*I am responsible for what I have not been*," says Georges Bernanos.)[3] In any fundamental unity in which a body-soul-and-spirit entelechy is constituted, the doors which had formerly been sealed begin to open wide. The capacities for thinking, feeling and volition emerge as interrelated, interconnected and coherent capacities rather than as compartmentalized and fractured skill sets or externalized techniques. Head, heart and hands in one place in one creature at one time, streaming in accord! Restored unity or even the movement toward restored unity constellates *a different kind of voice*. Something about the fundamental recovery of unity and coherence makes for a potentiated artistry. When reading Michael Martin, I am deeply struck by a uniquely potent and mature voice. There are millions and billions of precious human beings alive today, yet *this particular*, never-to-be-replaced or replicated father, spouse, poet, farmer, musician, carpenter and educator has grounded himself in the daily spiritual praxes of *metanoia* and *kenosis* and from them a new artistry has emerged. He is not ashamed of his commitments and relationships, whether to his family, the academy, the Earth, or the mystical body of Christ and through them, the word. He comes to philosophy and theology, the mystical and the corporeal, love and forgiveness, humility and awe, failure and virtue, poetry and prayer, the sacraments and the Eucharist *unashamedly*. They have formed him and he knows it and he is beholden to them.

In gradually intensifying years, his experience of the sacralization of time has blossomed out into the experience of space. Michael Martin's voice is intense and yet the attentive reader is invited into a spacious condition in which coercion is absent but the phenomena of grappling, questioning, and *sustained agapeic seeing, receiving and*

3. See Hans Urs von Balthasar, *Georges Bernanos: An Ecclesial Existence* (San Francisco: Communio Books–Ignatius Press, 1996).

125

giving are found on every page. Through his marriage and through the birth of his children, through the continual lyricism of the liturgical year, through the farming seasons of cultivation and harvesting, rest and activity, through the respiratory cycles of the academic year, we meet an author who has made choices. He has voluntarily chosen to walk the *metanoic* and *kenotic* paths, and in so doing, has voluntarily laid himself out to multiple forms of responsibility and radical layers of accountability. Instead of feeling burdened or confined by them, his choices have made him clear and in this clarity he shines. His orientation and structure have opened out into spiritual, emotional, psychological, and cultural space. The horizon line into which he invites the attentive reader is specific yet wide open, connected to and reflective of a sacramental relationship with creation, creatures and Creator. In this milieu, or living strata, any reader who arrives at his page is changed in the act of attentive reading. Because of the coherence in his voice, something like *a transmission* occurs in the act of reading *Poetic Word*. The reader is not filled with information. The reader experiences and is changed by experiencing.

During the gradual *metanoic* and *kenotic* processes of life, so central to Christian and to Roman Catholic formation, and so implicit in *The Poetic Word*, we have to first see and experience our individual and patterned shortcomings in order have the capacity to voluntarily choose to lay them down. This is usually a messy process. This gradual stripping away of the fruitless parts of ourselves happens in the milieu of love and forgiveness, the milieu of intimacy and disarmament, the metaphysical and existential geography where dying and becoming are intrinsically linked. In this milieu, we willingly let go of and die to layer after layer of who we have been in our various forms and conditions of habituated fragmentation. This simultaneous capacity for stripping away and paradoxical agapeic bridging are present in Michael Martin's poetic voice. The ways in which he draws near and enters into Plotinus, George Herbert, Robert Herrick, Martin Heidegger, and others makes this capacity for agapeic *presence of being* palpable to the attentive reader. Through the presence of the Master and in the communion of the saints, Michael Martin brings himself and his readers to experience humility and awe, warmth and substance, strength without violence, the luminous criteria that are generative and sacred. Without using the term fragmentation, St. Paul tells the Corinthians that if we do not have love, but continue speaking or acting, we find our (disconnected) selves in a hollowed out condition, banging as if a noisy gong.

Michael Martin comes from or abides in a different world, miles away from that fractured clanging in Corinthians. His words do not attribute any set of virtues to himself, or proclaim himself to have mastered love, but rather, through voluntary commitment, he stands disarmed, *walking his talk*. The poetic world he presents emerges as if unfurled, written in gold on a billowing page. He speaks from *within* sacramental embodiment and incarnational spirituality. Through an *agapeic spiritual practice*, shriven of competition, awakened through intentionality, embedded in phenomenology, irradiated by mystery, permeated by reverence, he discriminates and discerns *with* finesse and *through* love. The realm he discloses is one of genuine encounter, bridging transcendence and immanence. He traffics worlds, and *witnesses* artists, poets, philosophers, theologians and scientists through time and beyond, by virtue of a discerning agapeic intelligence of the heart. He brings his readers into sustained dialogue with his beloved friends, each of whom stream and shine through to those who are present: Plotinus, Simone Weil, John Milbank, Henri de Lubac, Goethe, Edmund Husserl, Georges Poulet, William Desmond, Hans Urs von Balthasar, Martin Heidegger, Edith Stein, George Herbert, Thomas Gallus, Thomas Aquinas, John Donne, Federico Garcia Lorca, Rudolf Steiner, Rainer Maria Rilke, Sergei Bulgakov, Robert Herrick, Nicholas and Mary Ferrar, Bernadette Soubirous, Gabriel Marcel, Gaston Bachelard, Jacques Maritain, Pseudo-Dionysius, David Jones, Franz Wright, Vladimir Solovyov, Alexander Blok, David Bohm, Henry Vaughn, Thomas Traherne, Novalis, Gerard Manley Hopkins, Teilhard de Chardin, Thomas Merton, William Everson, William Butler Yeats, and Joséphin Péladan. They are all here and remain alive.

Through them, what Michael Martin has to say about the contemplative tradition, cosmology, a radically Catholic re-imagination of life, being and world, the phenomenology of grace, the dislocating power of the poetic word, Goethean perception, and an epistemology of love bears immediate fruit. He also describes the hermeneutical cages, tribal reflexes and interpretive technologies that negatively impact being and life. His entry into religious experience, inexhaustible meaning, reverie, poetry, sacrament, opening, shimmering, shining splendor and metaphysical light speaks deeply about that of which *he knows by heart*. He has the courage to contrast those lights with a modernity in which "the dead forms multiply," in which we prefer career over vocation, in which the desiccating forms of scholarship interfere with or opportunistically manipulate phenomena, and in which the temptation to doctrinaire confessionalism and the infatuation with technology contribute to individual and collective fragmentation. Through the enstatic journey to grace, visual poems and the natural world, fallen stars and spiritual struggle, the music of the spheres and the language of the stars, altar and impanation, distrust of ceremony in contrast to the sacramental immanence that attends the Real Presence, Michael Martin invites readers to participate in and enter into an embodied, ensouled, incarnational Christian religious experience. The world of poetry, prophecy, and the poetic vocation which he inhabits is one of radiance and risk, controversy and courage, body and soul, the feminine and the sophianic, the arrival of the Beautiful. In Michael Martin, all of these are characterized by creative and transfigurative acts of adoration and prayer. By virtue of this agapeic capacity, *through the Rose to the Cross*, a practicing Catholic vitalized in a new and living way reminds us that "a poem is not a product," and that the great artist does not speak, but sings.

Readers who wonder about the present and future do well to do everything in their power to support the publisher Angelico Press, a house that has published three other ground-breaking and soul-searching volumes by the same author.[4] The Press has also presented a very significant body of work by authors of true significance and originality.

---

4. See Martin's *Meditations in Times of Wonder* (2014); *The Submerged Reality: Sophiology and the Turn to a Poetic Metaphysics*, with forward by Adrian Pabst, 2015; and *The Heavenly Country: An Anthology of Primary Sources, Poetry, and Critical Essays on Sophiology* (2016).

Afterword

The world needs Michael Martin's *The Incarnation of the Poetic Word* because it is a transformational work of rare artistry, intelligence, prayerfulness and depth. It is sensitively, accurately titled and subtitled (*Theological Essays on Poetry and Philosophy—Philosophical Essays on Poetry and Theology*). As a reader, drinking in the living quality of his work, his reception of the poetic word and path, I found myself changed, as if I had received a transfusion. Please, friends, stop and listen to an unashamedly sacramental, Catholic, and Eucharistic voice, because it is fiercely phenomenological, courageous, individuated, heart-felt, and generative. Thomas Merton and Anthony Bloom would both recognize the restored fundamental unity and coherence of Michael Martin's voice; there is someone there; there is someone home when he uses the pronoun "I." Surely they are singing for him from the far country. So should we, from the here and now!

THERESE SCHROEDER-SHEKER
Feast of the Transfiguration, 2016
The Chalice of Repose Project

Bibliography

Allen, Paul M. *Vladimir Soloviev: Russian Mystic.* Blauvelt, NY: Steiner, 1978.

Andrewes, Lancelot. *Ninety-Six Sermons.* 5 vols. Oxford: James Parker and Co., 1871–1875.

Apollinaire, Guillaume. *Bestiary, or The Parade of Orpheus.* Translated by Pepe Karmel. 1911; reprt. Boston: David R. Godine, 1980.

Aquinas, Thomas. *Catena Aurea: Commentary of the Four Gospels Collected out of the Works of the Fathers.* Four Volumes. 2nd edition. Oxford: John Henry and James Parker, 1864.

Asals, Heather A. L. *Equivocal Predication: George Herbert's Way to God.* Toronto: University of Toronto Press, 1981.

Bachelard, Gaston. *The Poetics of Reverie: Childhood, Language, and the Cosmos.* Translated by Daniel Russell. Boston: Beacon Press, 1969.

Baker, Augustine. *Holy Wisdom [Sancta Sophia] or Directions for the Prayer of Contemplation, Extracted out of more than Forty Treatises.* Digested by R. F. Serenus Cressy. Edited by Abbot Sweeney. New York: Harper & Brothers, 1950.

Balthasar, Hans Urs von. *Georges Bernanos: An Ecclesial Existence.* San Francisco: Communio Books–Ignatius Press, 1996.

———. *The Glory of the Lord: A Theological Aesthetics, Volume I: Seeing the Form.* Edited by Joseph Fessio, S.J. and John Riches. Translated by Leiva-Merikakis. San Francisco: Ignatius, 1982.

———. *The Glory of the Lord: A Theological Aesthetics, vol. 5: The Realm of Metaphysics in the Modern Age.* Translated by Oliver Davies et al. San Francisco: Ignatius Press, 1991.

Barfield, Owen. *Saving the Appearances: A Study in Idolatry.* 2nd edition. Middletown, CT: Wesleyan University Press, 1988.

Baxter, Richard. *A Christian Directory or Body of Practical Divinity.* London, 1677.

Bello, Angela Ales. *The Divine in Husserl and Other Explorations.* Translated by Anthony Calcagno. *Analecta Husserliana 98.* Edited by Anna-Teresa Tyminiecka. Dordrecht: Springer, 2012.

Benjamin, Walter. *Illuminations.* Edited with an introduction by Hannah Arendt. Translated by Harry Zohn. New York: Schocken Books, 1968.

Berdyaev, Nikolai. *The Meaning of the Creative Act*. Translated by Donald A. Lowrie. New York: Collier Books, 1962.

———. *The Fate of the Modern World*. Translated by Donald A. Lowrie. 1935; reprt., Ann Arbor, MI: The University of Michigan Press, 1961.

———. *Slavery and Freedom*. Translated by R.M. French. New York: Charles Scribner's Sons, 1944.

Blackstone, Bernard. "Story Books of Little Gidding: Wine and Poetry." *The Times Literary Supplement* (21 March 1936): 238.

Blake, William. *The Complete Poetry and Prose of William Blake*. Edited by David V. Erdman with commentary by Harold Bloom, revised edition. Berkeley and Los Angeles: University of California Press, 1982.

Bloch, Chana. *Spelling the Word: George Herbert and the Bible*. Berkeley: University of California Press, 1985.

Blok, Alexander. *Poems of Sophia*. Translated and edited by Boris Jakim. Kettering, OH: Semantron Press, 2014.

Bloom, Anthony (Metropolitan Anthony of Sourozh). *Beginning to Pray*. New York/Mahwah, NJ: Paulist Press, 1970.

———. *Courage to Pray*. Crestwood, NY: St. Vladimir Press, 1984.

———. *Living Prayer*. Springfield, IL: Templegate Publishers, 1966.

Bloom, Harold. *The Anxiety of Influence: A Theory of Poetry*. 2nd edition. New York: Oxford University Press, 1997.

Bulgakov, Sergius. *A Bulgakov Anthology: Sergius Bulgakov, 1871–1944*. Translated by Natalie Duddington and James Pain. Edited by James Pain and Nicolas Zernov. London: SPCK, 1976.

Clements, Arthur L. *Poetry of Contemplation: John Donne, George Herbert, Henry Vaughn and the Modern Period*. Albany: State University of New York Press, 1990.

Coolman, Boyd Taylor. "The Medieval Affective Dionysian Tradition." In *Rethinking Dionysius the Aeropagite*. Edited by Sarah Coakley and Charles M. Stang. Oxford: Wiley-Blackwell, 2009.

Crashaw, Richard. *The Poems, English, Latin and Greek of Richard Crashaw*. 2nd edition. Edited by L.C. Martin. Oxford: The Clarendon Press, 1957.

Davey, Richard. *The Pageant of London, Volume 2: AD 1500–1900*. London: Methuen & Co., 1906.

Desmond, William. *The Intimate Strangeness of Being: Metaphysics after Dialectic*. Washington, DC: The Catholic University of America Press, 2012.

———. *Is there a Sabbath for Thought?* Perspectives in Continental Philosophy. New York: Fordham University Press, 2005.

Dolan, Frances. *Whores of Babylon: Catholicism, Gender, and Seventeenth-Century Print Culture*. Ithaca and London: Cornell University Press, 1999.

Donne, John. *The Sermons of John Donne*. Edited by George R. Potter and Evelyn M. Simpson. 10 vols. Berkeley: University Press, 1972.

Eddington, A.S. *The Nature of the Physical World*. Cambridge: Cambridge University Press, 1928.

Elliot, T.S. *The Complete Poems and Plays, 1909–1950*. New York: Harcourt Brace Jovanovich, 1971.

———. *On Poetry and Poets*. New York: Farrar, Strauss & Giroux, 2009.

Ellrodt, Robert. *Seven Metaphysical Poets: A Structural Study of the Unchanging Self*. Oxford: Oxford University Press, 2000.

Eriugena, John Scotus. "Iohannis Scoti Eriugenae Expositiones in Ierarchiam Coelestem Corpus Christianorum." *Continuatio Mediaeualis* 31. Turnholt: Brepols, 1975.

Ettenhuber, Katrin. "The Preacher and Patristics." *The Oxford Handbook of the Early Modern Sermon*. Edited by Peter McCullough, Hugh Adlington, and Emma Rhatigan. Oxford: Oxford University Press, 2011.

———. *Donne's Augustine: Renaissance Culture of Interpretation*. Oxford: Oxford University Press, 2011.

Falque, Emmanuel. *God, the Flesh, and the Other: From Irenaeus to Duns Scotus*. Translated by William Christian Hackett. Evanston, IL: Northwestern University Press, 2015.

Ferrar, John and Doctor Jebb. *Nicholas Ferrar: Two Lives*. Cambridge: Cambridge University Press, 1855.

Florensky, Pavel. *The Pillar and Ground of Truth: An Essay in Orthodox Theodicy in Twelve Letters*. Princeton: Princeton University Press, 1997.

Gallagher, Catherine and Stephen Greenblatt. *Practicing New Historicism*. Chicago: The University of Chicago Press, 2000.

Gauchet, Marcel. *The Disenchantment of the World: A Political History of Religion*. Translated by Oscar Burge. Princeton: Princeton University Press, 1999.

Goethe, Johann Wolfgang von. *Scientific Studies (The Collected Works*, vol. 12). Princeton: Princeton University Press, 1995.

Greenblatt, Stephen. *Hamlet in Purgatory*. Princeton: Princeton University Press, 2001.

Grierson, Herbert J.C. (editor). *Metaphysical Lyrics and Poems of the Seventeenth Century: Donne to Butler*. Oxford: The Clarendon Press, 1921.

Guernsey, Julia Carolyn. *The Pulse of Praise: Form as a Second Self in the Poetry of George Herbert*. Cranbury, NJ: Assoc. Univ. Presses, 1999.

Guibbory, Achsah. *Ceremony and Community from Herbert to Milton: Literature, Religion, and Cultural Conflict in Seventeenth-Century England.* Cambridge: Cambridge University Press, 1998.

Haigh, Christopher. *English Reformations: Religion, Politics and Society under the Tudors.* Oxford: The Clarendon Press, 1993.

Hall, Thomas. *Funebria Floræ, the Downfall of May-Games...* 3rd edition, corrected. London, 1661.

Heidegger, Martin. *On the Way to Language.* Translated by Peter D. Hertz. New York: Harper Collins, 1971.

————. *The Phenomenology of Religious Life.* Studies in Continental Thought. Translated by Matthias Fritsch and Jennifer Anna Gosetti-Ferencei. Bloomington, IN: Indiana University Press, 2010.

————. *Poetry, Language, Thought.* Translated by Albert Hofstadter. New York: Harper & Row Publishers, 1971.

————. *The Question Concerning Technology and other Essays.* Translated by William Lovitt. New York: Harper Torchbooks, 1977.

Henry, Michel. *I Am the Truth: Toward a Philosophy of Christianity.* Translated by Susan Emanuel. Cultural Memory in the Present. Stanford: Stanford University Press, 2003.

————. Interviewed by Jean-Marie Brohm and Magali Uhl, "Art et phénoménologie de la vie (entretien, Montpellier, 1996)." In *Auto-donation: Entretiens et Conferences* by Michael Henry. 197–222. Paris: Editions Beauchesne, 2004.

Herbert, George. *The Works of George Herbert.* Edited by F. E. Hutchinson. Oxford: The Clarendon Press, 1941.

Herrick, Robert. *The Complete Poetry of Robert Herrick.* Edited by J. Max Patrick. New York: Norton, 1968.

————. *The Poetical Work of Robert Herrick.* Edited by L. C. Martin. Oxford: The Clarendon Press, 1956.

Heying, Charles. "Autonomy vs. Solidarity: Liberal, Totalitarian and Communitarian Traditions." *Administrative Theory & Praxis* 21, no. 1 (March 1999): 39–50.

Hooker, Richard. *The Lawes of Ecclesiastical Politie.* London, 1594–97.

Hungerford, Anthony. *The Advise of a Sonne, Now Professing the Religion Established in the present Church of England, to his deare Mother, yet a Roman Catholike.* Oxford, 1616.

Husserl, Edmund. *Cartesian Meditations: An Introduction to Phenomenology.* Translated by Dorion Cairns. The Hague: Martinus Nijhoff, 1960.

————. *Ideas Pertaining to a Pure Phenomenology and to a Phenomeno-*

logical Philosophy, First Book: General Introduction to a Pure Phenomenology. Translated by F. Kersten. The Hague: Springer, 1982.

Hutton, Ronald. *The Rise and Fall of Merry England: The Ritual Year 1400–1700.* Oxford: Oxford University Press, 1996.

Jaegerschmid, Adelgundis. "Conversations with Edmund Husserl, 1931–1938." Translated by Marcus Brainard. *New Yearbook for Phenomenology and Phenomenological Philosophy* 1 (2001): 331–50.

Janicaud, Dominique. *Phenomenology "Wide Open": After the French Debate.* Translated by Charles N. Cabral. New York: Fordham University Press, 2005.

Johnston, Sarah Iles. "Religious Practices of the Home and the Family: Rome." In *Religions of the Ancient World: A Guide.* General edition. Cambridge: Harvard University Press, 2004.

Kelly, Robert. *The Convections.* Santa Barbara, CA: Black Sparrow Press, 1978.

Kimmey, John L. "Order and Form in Herrick's *Hesperides.*" *The Journal of English and Germanic Philology* 70, no.1 (April 1971): 255–68.

Laud, William. *The Works of the Most Reverend Father in God, William Laud. D.D., sometime Lord Archbishop of Canterbury: Volume IV: History of Troubles and Trial, &c.* Oxford: John Henry Parker, 1854.

Leclerq, Jean. *The Love of Learning and the Desire for God: A Study of Monastic Culture.* Translated by Catharine Misrahi. New York: Fordham University Press, 1961.

Lloyd, David. *Memories of the Lives, Actions, Sufferings & Deaths of Those Noble, Reverend, and Excellent Personages that Suffered by Death, Sequestration, Decimation, or Otherwise for the Protestant Religion...* London, 1668.

Lorca, Federico Garcia. *Poet in New York.* Translated by Ben Belitt. New York: Grove Press, 1955.

Lubac, Henri de. *Surnaturel: Études Historiques.* Paris: Aubier, 1946.

Luckyi, Christina. "Disciplining the Mother in Seventeenth-Century English Puritanism." *Performing Maternity in Early Modern England.* Edited by Kathryn M. Moncrief and Kathryn R. McPherson, Studies in Performance and Early Modern Drama. 101–14. Aldershot, UK: Ashgate, 2007.

Manoussakis, John P. "The Phenomenon of God: From Husserl to Marion." *American Catholic Philosophical Quarterly* 78, no. 1 (2004): 53–68.

Marcel, Gabriel. *The Mystery of Being 2: Faith and Reality.* Translated by René Hague. Chicago: Henry Regnery Company, 1960.

Marcus, Leah S. "Conviviality Interrupted or, Herrick and Postmodernism." *Lords of Wine and Oil*, 65–82.

Marion, Jean-Luc. *In Excess: Studies of Saturated Phenomena*. Translated by Robyn Horner and Vincent Berraud. New York: Fordham University Press, 2001.

———. *Prolegomena to Charity*. Translated by Stephen Lewis. New York: Fordham University Press, 2002.

Maritain, Jacques. *Art and Poetry*. Translated by Elva de P. Matthews. New York: Philosophical Library, 1943.

Marshall, Peter. *Beliefs and the Dead in Reformation England*. Oxford: Oxford University Press, 2002.

Martin, Michael (editor). *The Heavenly Country: An Anthology of Primary Sources, Poetry, and Critical Essays on Sophiology*. Kettering, OH: Angelico Press/Sophia Perennis, 2016.

———. *Literature and the Encounter with God in Post-Reformation England*. Farnham, U.K: Ashgate Publishing, 2014.

Martz. *The Poetry of Meditation: A Study in English Religious Literature of the Seventeenth Century*. 2nd edition. New Haven: Yale University Press, 1962.

Maycock, A.L. *Nicholas Ferrar of Little Gidding*. 1938; reprt. Grand Rapids, MI: William B. Eerdmans Publishing Company, 1980.

Merleau-Ponty, Maurice. *The Visible and the Invisible, followed by Working Notes*. Edited by Claude Lefort. Translated by Alphonso Lingis. Evanston, IL: Northwestern University Press, 1968.

Merton, Thomas. *The Inner Experience: Notes on Contemplation*. Edited with an introduction by William Shannon. San Francisco: HarperSanFrancisco, 2003.

Midgley, Mary. *Science as Salvation: A Modern Myth and Its Meaning*. London: Routledge, 1992.

Milbank, John. *The Suspended Middle: Henri de Lubac and the Debate concerning the Supernatural*. Grand Rapids, MI: William B. Eerdmans, 2005.

Miller, Adam. "Badiou, Marion, and St. Paul: Immanent Grace." *Continuum Studies in Continental Philosophy*. London: Continuum, 2008.

More, Thomas. *Utopia*. Translated and edited by Robert M. Adams, revised, 2nd edition. Norton Critical Editions in the History of Ideas. New York: W.W. Norton & Company, 1992.

Nancy, Jean-Luc. *Adoration: The Deconstruction of Christianity II*. Translated by John McKeane, Perspectives in Continental Philosophy. New York: Fordham University Press, 2013.

Netzley, Ryan. *Reading, Desire, and the Eucharist in Early Modern Reli-*

gious Poetry. Toronto: University of Toronto Press, 2011.

Nietzsche, Friedrich. *The Use and Abuse of History.* Translated by Adrian Collins. Indianapolis, IN: Library of Liberal Arts, 1949.

———. "The Will to Power." Translated by J.M. Kennedy. Edited by Oscar Levy. Vol 9. *The Complete Works of Friedrich Nietzsche.* Edinburgh: T.N. Foulis, 1913.

Novalis. *Hymns to the Night.* Translated by Dick Higgins. Revised edition. New York: McPherson & Company, 1984.

Oley, Barnabas. "A Prefatory View of the Life of Mr. Geo. Herbert, &c" in G.H. [George Herbert], *A Priest to the Temple, or The Country Parson His Character and Rule of Holy Life.* London, 1652.

Patrides, C.A. Introduction, *The English Poems of George Herbert.* London: J.M. Dent, 1974.

Pearson, Irene. "Raphael as Seen by Russian Writers from Zhukovsky to Turgenev." *Slavonic and East European Review* 39, no. 3 (July 1981): 346–69.

Péladan, Joséphin. *La Decadence esthetique: L'art ochlocratique, salons de 1882 et 1883.* Paris: Camille Dalou, 1888.

———. *L'Art Idéaliste & Mystique: Doctrine de l'Ordre et du Salon Annuel des Rose+Croix,* 2nd edition. Paris: Chamuel, 1894.

Plotinus. *The Enneads.* Translated by Stephen MacKenna and B.S. Page. New York: Penguin, 1991.

Polanyi, Karl. *The Great Transformation.* Boston: Beacon Press, 1957.

Poulet, Georges. "The Phenomenology of Reading." *New Literary History* 1 no. 1 (1969): 53–68.

Pseudo-Dionysius. *The Complete Works.* Translated by Colm Luibheid and Paul Rorem. New York: Paulist Press, 1987.

Rabil Jr., Albert. *Erasmus and the New Testament: The Mind of a Christian Humanist.* San Antonio, TX: Trinity University Press, 1972.

Ransome, Joyce. *The Web of Friendship: Nicholas Ferrar and Little Gidding.* London: James Clarke & Co., 2011.

Reed, John Shelton. "'A Female Movement': The Feminization of Nineteenth-Century Anglo-Catholicism," *Anglican and Episcopal History* 57, no. 2 (June 1988): 199–238.

Richey, Esther Gillman. "The Intimate Other: Lutheran Subjectivity in Spencer, Donne, and Herbert." In *Modern Philology* 108, no. 3 (February 2011): 343–74.

Rickey, Mary Ellen. *Utmost Art: Complexity in the Verse of George Herbert.* Lexington: University of Kentucky Press, 1966.

Rorty, Richard. *Philosophy and Social Hope.* London: Penguin, 1999.

Ruusbroec, John. *The Spiritual Espousals and Other Works.* Translated by James A. Wiseman. Mahwah, N.J.: Paulist Press, 1986.

Schoenfeldt, Michael. *Prayer and Power: George Herbert and Renaissance Courtship.* Chicago: University of Chicago Press, 1991.

Schwartz, Regina M. *Sacramental Poetics at the Dawn of Secularism: When God Left the World,* Cultural Memory in the Present. Stanford: Stanford University Press, 2008.

Scruton, Roger. *The Soul of the World.* Princeton: Princeton University Press, 2014.

Shakespeare, William. *The Riverside Shakespeare.* Edited by G. Blakemore and J.J.M. Tobin. 2nd edition. Boston: Houghton Mifflin Company, 1997.

Shelley, Percy Bysshe. *Shelley's Poetry and Prose.* Edited by Neil Fraistat and Donald H. Reiman, Norton Critical Editions. New York: W.W. Norton and Company, 1977.

Sidney, Phillip Sir. *Sir Philip Sidney's An Apology for Poetry and Apostrophil and Stella: Texts and Contexts.* Edited by Peter C. Herman. Glen Allen, VA: College Publishing, 2001.

Solovyov, Sergey Fr. *Vladimir Solovyov: His Life and Creative Evolution.* Translated by Aleksey Gibson. Fairfax, VA: Eastern Christian Publications, 2000.

Solovyov, Vladimir. *The Religious Poetry of Vladimir Solovyov.* Edited by Boris Jakim. Kettering, OH: Semantron Press, 2014.

St. Bonaventure. *The Life of St. Francis.* London: J.M. Dent and Company, 1904.

Staiger, Emil. *Basic Concepts of Poetics.* Edited by Marianne Burkhard and Luanne T. Frank. Translated by Janette C. Hudson and Luanne T. Frank. Park, PA: The Pennsylvania University Press, 1991.

Stein, Arnold. *George Herbert's Lyrics.* Baltimore, MD: The John Hopkins University Press, 1968.

Stein, Edith. *The Science of the Cross. The Collected Works of Edith Stein.* Volume 6. Translated by Josephine Koeppel. Washington, DC: ICS Publications, 2002.

———. *Knowledge and Faith.* Translated by Walter Redmond. Washington DC: ICS Publications, 2000.

Steiner, Rudolf. *The Arts and Their Mission.* Translated by Lisa D. Monges and Virginia Moore. Spring Valley, NY: Anthroposophic Press, 1964.

Strier, Richard. *Love Known: Theology and Experience in George Herbert's Poetry.* Chicago: The University of Chicago Press, 1991.

———. "George Herbert and Ironic Ekphrasis." *Classical Philology* 102, no. 1 (January 2007): 96–109.

Summers, Joseph H. *George Herbert: His Religion and Art*. Cambridge: Harvard University Press, 1968.

Swardson, H. R. "Herrick and the Ceremony of Mirth," in *Poetry and the Fountain of Light: Observations on the Conflict between Christian and Classical Traditions in Seventeenth-Century Poetry*. Columbia: University of Missouri Press, 1962.

Targoff, Ramie. *Common Prayer: The Language of Public Devotion in Early Modern English*. Chicago: The University of Chicago Press, 2001.

Taylor, Charles. *Sources of the Self: The Making of the Modern Identity*. Cambridge: Harvard University Press, 1989.

———. *A Secular Age*. Cambridge: Belknap-Harvard University Press, 2012.

Taylor, Jeremy. *The Whole Works of the Right Rev. Jeremy Taylor, D.D.* Edited by Reginald Heber and Rev. Charles Page Eden. 10 vols. London: Longmans, Green & Co., 1883.

Teilhard de Chardin, Pierre. *Writings in Time of War*. Translated by René Hague. New York: Harper & Row, Publishers, 1968.

Thompson, E. P. *The Making of the English Working Class*. 1963. Reprint. Harmondsworth: Penguin, 1986.

Troyes, Chrétien de. *Le Roman de Perceval, ou Le Conte du Graal*. Edited by William Roach. Genève: Librarie Droz, 1959.

Tuve, Rosemond. *A Reading of George Herbert*. Chicago: University of Chicago Press, 1952.

Tvordi, Jessica. "The Poet in Exile: Robert Herrick and the 'loathed Country-life." *Rural Space in the Middle Ages and Early Modern Age: The Spatial Turn in Pre-Modern Studies*. Edited by J. Max Patrick and Christopher R. Clason. 295–318. Berlin: De Gruyter, 2012.

Vaughn, Henry. *The Complete Poems of Henry Vaughn*. Edited by French Fogle. The Stuart Editions. New York: New York University Press, 1965.

Wahl, Jean. *Poésie, Pensée, Perception*. Paris: Calmann-Lévy, 1948.

Walsham, Alexandra. *Providence in Early Modern England*. Oxford: Oxford University Press, 1999.

Walzer, Michael. *The Revolution of the Saints: A Study in the Origins of Radical Politics*. Cambridge: Harvard University Press, 1965.

Weil, Simone. *Waiting for God*. Translated by Emma Craufurd. 1951. Reprint. New York: Harper Perennial, 2009.

White, James Boyd. *"The Book of Starres": Learning to Read George Herbert*. Ann Arbor: University of Michigan Press, 1994.

Wordsworth, Christopher. *Ecclesiastical Biography; or Lives of Eminent Men connected with the History of Religion in England; from the Commencement of the Reformation to the Revolution*, 6 vols. London: F.C. and J. Rivington, 1810.

Yeats, William Butler. *Ideas of Good and Evil*, 3rd ed. London: A.H. Bullen, 1907.

Young, R.V. *Doctrine and Devotion in the Seventeenth-Century Poetry: Studies in Donne, Herbert, Crashaw and Vaughn*. Studies in Renaissance Literature. Cambridge: D.S. Brewer, 2000.

Zajonc, Arthur. "Attending to Interconnection, Living the Lesson." *The Heart of Higher Education: A Call to Renewal. Transforming the Academy through Collegial Conversations* by Parker J. Palmer and Arthur Zajonc, with Megan Scribner. San Francisco: Josey-Bass, 2010.

Made in the USA
Lexington, KY
27 January 2017